FAILURES OF FORGIVENESS

FAILURES
OF
FORGIVENESS

WHAT WE GET WRONG AND
HOW TO DO BETTER

MYISHA CHERRY

PRINCETON UNIVERSITY PRESS

PRINCETON *&* OXFORD

Published by Princeton University Press
41 William Street, Princeton, New Jersey 08540
99 Banbury Road, Oxford OX2 6JX

press.princeton.edu

Library of Congress Control Number: 2022950457

ISBN 9780691223193
ISBN (e-book) 9780691230474

British Library Cataloging-in-Publication Data is available

Editorial: Rob Tempio, Chloe Coy
Jacket: Katie Osborne
Production: Erin Suydam
Publicity: Maria Whelan, Carmen Jimenez

This book has been composed in Arno Pro

Printed on acid-free paper. ∞

Printed in the United States of America

10 9 8 7 6 5 4 3 2 1

In memory of
Charles Mills.
A brilliant mind,
a generous mentor,
and the funniest man
in philosophy.
I will forever miss you
(and your handouts)!

CONTENTS

FAILURES OF FORGIVENESS

INTRODUCTION

FORGIVENESS AND MAGICAL THINKING

ON JUNE 17, 2015, the white supremacist Dylann Roof committed what many would call an unforgivable crime. During a Bible study at Emanuel African Methodist Episcopal Church in Charleston, South Carolina, he murdered nine Black churchgoers. The shooting and the subsequent courtroom events gripped the nation not only because of the horrific nature of the crime but also because of the way in which some members of the victims' families responded to Roof. They forgave him.

At Roof's first court appearance, Nadine Collier, the daughter of seventy-year-old victim Ethel Lance, said, "You took something very precious from me. I will never talk to her again. I will never, ever hold her again. But I forgive you. God have mercy on your soul." Anthony Thompson, the husband of slain Myra Thompson, forgave Roof and implored him to repent and confess. Bethane Middleton-Brown, the sister of Rev. DePayne Middleton-Doctor, acknowledged her anger in the courtroom but expressed her sister's commitment to love over hate: "She taught me that we are the families that love built. We have no room for hate, so we have to forgive." Bethane forgave Roof, as would Felicia Sanders, the mother of Tywanza Sanders. As Bethane told Roof at his sentencing in 2017, "I wanted to hate you, but my faith tells me no. I wanted to remain angry and bitter, but my view of life won't let me."

Despite the slaughter of their family members in a sacred and safe space by a man whom the victims had welcomed, the bereaved found it in their hearts to forgive. Many of us witnessing the case could not imagine that we would do the same. Surely, we have withheld forgiveness from people for transgressions far less serious. Even the most pious of bystanders would have understood the families' refusal to forgive. And yet, some resisted hatred and publicly forgave.

With resentment and revenge so rampant in Western culture, these forgivers deserve our praise for their unconditional act. Perhaps they could teach us something about forgiveness. Following the courtroom statements, many editorial columns across the country suggested as much, with headlines like "Hate Won't Win" and "How 'Emanuel' Reveals the Power of Forgiveness."

In response to what took place at Emanuel, I became overwhelmed by grief, sadness, and anger. Soon after, reading the media's coverage of the families, I was overtaken by worry. I was troubled by the fact that forgiveness was being depicted as something magical—enchanted words that once spoken and performed could immediately heal wounds and racism. Less was said about what it took for the family members to forgive and continue on that path.

In addition, even though the case is an example of extraordinary acts of forgiveness, not every family member or person in attendance responded with a forgiving stance. Who were they and why did they decide to withhold forgiveness? Weren't their stories worth hearing too? I was bothered by the fact that the media were using the word "forgiveness" with no attention to what it meant, what it didn't mean, what forgiveness required, and what our role was as community members in helping to make forgiveness a reality. I was also worried that outsiders would use Nadine's and Anthony's forgiveness to force other people to forgive. If those in Charleston could forgive Roof, clearly you should forgive me!

My sense is that while many were inspired by these individuals' willingness to forgive, fewer were inspired to curb and halt hatred and violence. We were praising and promoting forgiveness, yet taking its meaning for granted. Part of the problem had to do with our narrow definition, amplified in popular culture. It's akin to the endings of certain Hollywood films—desirable results have been achieved, good has prevailed over evil, and positive emotions win the day. Similarly, we tend to depict forgiveness as a feel-good act that can provide a happy resolution for all those involved. Forgiveness is the thing that helps us ride off into the sunset together, always!

All of us have either forgiven or received forgiveness. And many of us believe it has some moral value, even if we disagree about what that value is. We tend to think that we know, somewhat naturally, what forgiveness is and how to use it well. This helps explain why when I meet a person for the first time and tell them that I write about forgiveness, they immediately and confidently share their thoughts about the subject. Forgiveness is such a central and prevalent practice in our social world, how could we fail to understand it? Social media quotations echo claims about the psychological benefits of forgiveness; businesses promote it as a workplace value; and, as we've seen, newspaper reporters praise victims and their families for extending it to seemingly unworthy candidates. We often beg for and expect it from family and friends—thinking forgiveness alone, or at least primarily, can solve our interpersonal problems.

In the wake of the Charleston tragedy, the power of forgiveness was quickly becoming exaggerated. To be sure, forgiveness is powerful. But it's not magical. It doesn't work on its own, nor does it transform states of affairs in an instant. And just as with any other power, we can misuse it, thereby causing more hurt. As I watched these events unfold in the media, I knew that what was needed was a demystification of forgiveness—an account of its powers and limitations, and how we might do better as extenders, promoters, and withholders of forgiveness. To discover those answers for myself, I decided to write this book.

We think that forgiveness is the "letting go" of negative feelings. It aims at reconciliation and is necessary to build a better future. It is what the mature extend and what the bitter hold back. We think promoting it is always a virtue, and discouraging it is a vice. As I hope to convince you over the course of this book, we could not be more misguided.

This narrow view of forgiveness is one with which I was intimately acquainted. I grew up constantly hearing "Let it go" as a religious command and wise advice from Christian ministers and older community members. As a child, I was taught that holding on to anger wasn't "pretty." However, I began to notice that something wasn't quite right with the way religious leaders, self-help gurus, journalists, my elders, and my peers were talking about forgiveness. The coverage surrounding the Charleston massacre, which occurred as I was entering graduate school, was the straw that broke the camel's back and compelled me to focus my research on forgiveness. During that time, I encountered perspectives about forgiveness that were drastically different from what I'd been taught growing up and what I was witnessing in the media. From the work of the eighteenth-century British moralist Joseph Butler, I discovered that we can forgive and yet remain angry. From contemporary feminist philosophers such as Kathryn Norlock and Alice MacLachlan, I learned that forgiveness doesn't require rigid conditions. Others, such as the ethicist Charles Griswold, taught me that forgiveness could be done well or badly. I was discovering like-minded thinkers—folks who, like me, were not satisfied with our prevailing picture of forgiveness.

Now, as a philosopher, self-proclaimed "public defender" of anger, and proud withholder of forgiveness, I believe it is time to draw back the curtain so that we can see forgiveness in a new light. On the broader view of forgiveness that I propose in this book, forgiveness is not one thing, nor does it aim at one goal; and it is not without its limitations. This new way of thinking about forgiveness, I'll argue, challenges how we often talk and think about it, as well as how we go about recovering from wrongdoing. Frankly put, the narrow view doesn't do anyone any good. I hope to show you that the broader view does.

I will explore how this more expansive understanding of forgiveness can help us improve in our roles as requesters, encouragers, and recipients of forgiveness, as well as forgivers and withholders of forgiveness. I'll examine how such improvements can make it more likely that we will repair our relationships, communities, and our lives. The type of repair that I will challenge us to seek is *radical repair*. Radical repair addresses the roots of a problem, aims for change, and requires everyone—not just the victim—to help make things right. Those who participate in radical repair accept that some things may never return back to their original state, but that trying is worth the effort. I will also demonstrate how a narrow view of forgiveness can have a negative impact on the above roles, making radical repair less likely. Even when we have a more expansive view of forgiveness, however, I'll argue that we can still misuse our powers of forgiveness. The effect of the narrow view and the tendency for us to misuse our powers show why it is necessary for us to retrain ourselves. This retraining involves thinking differently about forgiveness and doing forgiveness better.

In this book, then, I do not merely aim to offer a better understanding of forgiveness. Instead, I will show how we can make better use of forgiveness, recognize when we are wielding it in ways that are abusive and oppressive, and accept its limitations. I will outline just how and why we should rethink the ways we respond to wrongdoing.

We all navigate the complicated paths of relationships, emotions, conflict, tough conversations, and solidarity. And many of us have been victimized by those who have vowed to never hurt us. We've witnessed wrongdoings by others or have ourselves wronged others. This book speaks broadly to all of us as we grapple with the aftermath of wrongdoing and seek out ways to help repair our world. This book is about victims. But it is also about wrongdoers, family, friends, religious leaders, psychologists, and journalists.

I am going to take you into courtrooms and truth commissions to examine what goes wrong when we encourage forgiveness with a narrow view. I'll delve into our private lives to examine the philosophical and social factors that influence our own unreasonable expectations of forgiveness, including our beliefs about who should give it, when they should give it, and why.

I'll examine obstacles that a refusal to forgive poses to familial bonds by considering whether we have a duty to forgive family members. Is a lack of forgiveness compatible with love? And why does the long shadow of wrongdoing make personal reparative attempts both difficult and, at times, impossible?

I'll take you into the workplace to examine the appropriateness of forgiveness in a professional context. I'll take you to press conferences in the aftermath of police violence to talk about how publicly inquiring about forgiveness ends up disrespecting victims by rushing and coercing them to forgive. I'll challenge the ways in which we criticize both those who forgive and those who refuse to forgive.

In the pages that follow, I will wrestle on a personal and intellectual level with forgiveness. And, I admit, I am still wrestling. I know I am not alone. I hope what I've discovered can be of use to you on your own journey. In the end, I believe you will have a better understanding of your own relationship with forgiveness—when you are willing to offer or ask for it, and why. And you will be able to use it more wisely—for radical repair.

1

WHAT TO EXPECT WHEN YOU ARE EXPECTING FORGIVENESS

IT WAS JANUARY 2006. But it seems like only yesterday that my stepfather found my fifty-four-year-old mother unresponsive in their Delaware home and rushed her to the hospital. I was living in Maryland at the time; my older sister was living in Mississippi. We, her only children, hurried to be by our mother's side. Initially, seeing what we believed was progress, we were hopeful. She had survived several operations, was going through dialysis, and was able to talk with us softly. I can still vividly see her laughing at a joke my sister told as we gathered around her hospital bed.

But her recovery would prove short-lived. By September my mother moved into a hospice. Naive about hospices in general, I remained hopeful, even though my sister instructed me to bring a suit on this trip. After spending the night in her room—falling asleep to the MTV music awards—I woke up alone to my mother's cold, pale body. She was gone. Shaking, in shock, and heartbroken, I somehow managed to dial my sister's number to tell her the news. Although I would often find a way to hide or suppress it in the ensuing months and years, the grief hit me hard. My feelings of loss were compounded by what my sister and I soon discovered about our stepfather.

During the final months of my mother's life, my stepfather had done the unthinkable. While my mother lay in a hospital bed fighting for her life, he brought another woman into their home. It was not a one-night stand. She moved in. My sister and I were furious. How could he disrespect my mother and our family? How could he forsake her when she needed him the most? How could he "love" another woman at a time when my mother needed to feel every ounce of his love?

The day of my mother's funeral, he humbly came to me to apologize and beg for my forgiveness. I dismissed the gesture. I told him that it was something he needed to address with my deceased mother and his god. Those were the last words I have spoken to him. My sister, on the other hand, has remained in contact with him over the years.

I recently received several text messages from my family alerting me that my stepfather wanted my phone number and asking me whether they had permission to share it with him. The text messages sent my blood boiling, resurfacing feelings of anger that I thought had disappeared years ago. I declined his request, and my sister scolded me for my unwillingness to speak to him after more than a decade of silence. "You know you should forgive," she said. I suspect that many members of my family would agree with my sister's assessment. While she had let go of her anger and resumed communicating with our step-father, I appeared bitter and distant.

As strange as this might sound, I believe that I *have* forgiven him. Of course, my forgiveness looks different from my sister's, and one reason it is difficult for my sister to recognize my for-giveness is that she holds the common yet limited view of for-giveness. For many, to forgive means to reconcile, to let go of anger. Anything that falls outside of that paradigm is seldom counted as forgiveness. And it's not just my sister who holds this narrow view. This is the prevailing view of forgiveness in our society. If asked what it means to forgive, many of us describe it as involving the release of anger and other negative attitudes. Expanding our thinking about forgiveness means absorbing just how prevalent this limited view is in our society. In the end, I trust that you will eventually discard and replace this restricted conception with a perspective that can help you expand and improve your expectations of forgiveness and of one another.

THE NARROW VIEW

To begin to understand what I call the narrow view of forgiveness, consider how DeVon Franklin, Hollywood producer of inspirational films like *The Pursuit of Happyness*, describes forgiving his father.[1] As a result of an unhealthy lifestyle, including heavy drinking, Franklin's father died an early death, leaving Franklin fatherless, empty, and angry. He soon found himself projecting this anger onto others. He recalls that forgiving his father involved letting go of anger. Franklin admits, "It wasn't easy, because sometimes we can find comfort in our anger, our frustration, our bitterness that comes from unforgiveness." Recognizing what can happen when you don't forgive, he notes: "When I hold on to resentment, I am the one who bears the weight of it."[2]

We witness the tight connection between forgiveness and compassion in the actions of Pope John Paul II. After he was shot in St. Peter's Square in 1981, he forgave his would-be assassin by refusing to treat him with contempt. The man was convicted and sentenced to life in prison. Eventually Pope John

Paul II visited the prisoner, comforted him, and told him he was "sincerely forgiven."³ In 2000 the shooter was granted a pardon at the pope's request.

Martin Luther King Jr. took a similar stance of forgiveness toward Izola Currey, a forty-two-year-old woman who stabbed him in 1958. The blade rested on his aorta, and doctors believed that if King had so much as sneezed, it would have caused a fatal puncture. Rather than feeling disregard or contempt toward his attacker, King responded with kindness and generosity: "I felt no ill will toward Mrs. Izola Currey and know that thoughtful people will do all in their power to see that she gets the help she apparently needs if she is to become a free and constructive member of society."⁴

Similar connections, concerning forgiveness and hatred, are often heard in the response of family members of victims of violent crime. When the Green River serial killer was finally caught and sentenced for the 1980s killings of forty-nine women, his victims' families were given an opportunity to speak in court. The father of sixteen-year-old victim Linda Rule read a statement that embodied the idea of forgiveness as the letting go of hatred. "Mr. Ridgway," Robert Rule said, "there are people here that hate you. I am not one of them. I forgive you for what you have done. You are forgiven, Sir." Just as it did for Bethane Middleton-Brown—the sister of one of Dylann Roof's victims—forgiveness, for Rule, involved letting go of hatred toward the wrongdoer.

Although they differ from each other in many ways, the stories point to a similar, popular view of forgiveness, and they are inspiring because the victims chose to respond with loving emotions in the face of evil and callousness. Forgiveness, on this view, is primarily a matter of emotions and attitudes. To forgive is to let go of negative emotions, like anger and hatred, and replace them with more positive emotions, like compassion and love. So understood, forgiveness is valuable because such emotions will affect our behavior. It will orient us to avoid seeking retribution and to engage, instead, in compassionate or reconciliatory action.

As a result, many of us are prone to think that forgiveness *always* involves these emotions, attitudes, and actions. We expect forgivers to give up their anger. If they do not, we are likely to conclude that they have not forgiven. We expect a forgiver to respond to the wrongdoer with compassion. If she does not, we are likely to think that she has not truly forgiven. (And we expect a forgiving stepdaughter to reconcile with her stepfather. If she does not, we are likely to think that she has not "let it go.")

This general way of thinking about forgiveness is also popular among philosophers, who often claim that forgiveness involves giving up negative attitudes, though they disagree about which attitudes, precisely, need to go. The most common views tend to focus on anger, contempt, and hatred. I'm sure many of you can identify with at least one of these views.

The forgiveness accounts of Bethane Middleton-Brown and DeVon Franklin share similarities with the most popular version of the narrow view of forgiveness—as the giving up of anger. Philosophers who hold this view—call them *anger eradicators*—believe that forgiveness is the giving up of vindictive passions such as anger and resentment. Forgiveness is a matter of how I *feel* about you, rather than a matter of how I *treat* you. When other people wrong us, they send the message that we do not matter. Resentment is a response that communicates that we do not accept this message.[5] To forgive, according to anger eradicators, is to overcome this resentment, to no longer respond to the wrongdoer with resentful feelings.

When a victim overcomes her resentment, this does not mean that she accepts the message that she does not matter. Nor does it mean that she is no longer bothered by the message. Instead, it simply means that the victim no longer harbors angry feelings toward the offender, is not reliving the past, and is not dwelling in the feeling that they've been hurt. For some anger eradicators, it is appropriate (although not required, nor always possible) for the victim to overcome resentment when the wrongdoer gives her moral reasons to do so. These reasons may include admitting the wrongdoing and disavowing the message their wrongdoing communicated.

Other philosophers—call them *anger moderators*—take seriously the need to manage rather than give up anger through forgiveness. For anger moderators, forgiveness is a refusal to be dominated by anger. We can imagine what it's like to be dominated by anger. We can feel anger so often that it gets in the way of meaningful pursuits. We might feed it by constantly thinking of the wrongdoing; project it on to others; or use it to inspire vengeful or self-destructive acts. Forgiveness involves a refusal of these actions. Why not get rid of anger entirely? For anger moderators, it's because some anger—anger that expresses a hatred for vice and love of virtue—plays an important, positive role in our lives. It's a way to express self-respect and bear witness to wrongdoing and oppression. It can also motivate us to engage in social change. A vicious, unmoderated anger can make us thirsty for revenge, but virtuous anger is different. What we should give up through forgiveness, then, is this unmoderated anger.

Other philosophers think that in addition to anger, we should give up contempt, as Martin Luther King Jr. and Pope John Paul II once did. Let's call these philosophers *contempt eradicators.* For these thinkers, if a victim has given up resentment but still has contempt for the wrongdoer, he cannot be said to have forgiven. In contrast to resentment, which is merely the attitude that one has been wronged, contempt, as one philosopher recently defined it, is a "dismissive and insulting attitude that manifests disregard for its target."[6] When we have contempt for a person, we think of them as beneath us and we treat them as worthless. There is nothing special about resentment that would make it the only emotion to overcome through forgiveness. Rather, both contempt *and* resentment separate us from one another. That is why, according to contempt eradicators, to forgive, we must overcome both resentment *and* contempt.

A final group of eradicators follows Bethane Middleton-Brown and Robert Rule, who expressed the idea that forgiveness necessitates the letting go of hatred. For *hatred eradicators,* forgiveness involves giving up resentment *and* hatred.[7] The victim, according to hatred eradicators, does not give up her judgment of the wrongdoing when she forgives. Instead, she revises her judgment of the offender. Forgiveness, then, occurs when the victim decides to see the offender in a new light. It occurs when, according to the philosopher Jean Hampton in *Forgiveness and Mercy,* the victim decides to "wash away . . . the immoral . . . character traits in her ultimate judgment of him . . . and comes to see [the offender] as still decent, not rotten as a person."[8] This letting go of hatred paves the way for a transformation in the relationship.

According to Roof's hateful manifesto, he held contempt for Blacks and hoped his actions would spark a race war. Although he saw Blacks as inferior, his forgivers refused to return the same sentiment. Words and phrases heard in the courtroom—such as "Repent," "I pray God on your soul," and "May God have mercy on you"—provide evidence that some victims were committed to giving up hatred. And they saw their forgiveness as constituting such an act.

So far we've seen that philosophical accounts of forgiveness include the letting go of negative emotions and attitudes like anger, contempt, and hatred. But there are also those who claim that forgiveness involves not just overcoming certain attitudes but also forgoing vengeful actions and extending goodwill.

Joseph Butler, the eighteenth-century British moralist, may not be as famous as Socrates or Aristotle, but his thinking on forgiveness and anger has been quite influential. In a series of sermons delivered to a packed audience at Rolls Chapel in London in 1726, Butler laid out a provocative view of forgiveness. According to Butler, in forgiveness the victim *extends* compassion, pity, and goodwill toward the offender. Let's call those who think like Butler the *goodwill extenders*. What a person doesn't *give up* when they forgive is a moderated form of resentment. (The anger moderators borrow this insight from Butler.) The act of moderating resentment entails having a proportionate degree of resentment. But it also includes using resentment not for revenge but for justice, and not acting in malice. Moderation involves having the right balance of compassion and displeasure toward the offender. This moderation of resentment through forgiveness, Butler argued, is not contrary to love or benevolence. We can love our enemies and yet have resentment against them for the wrongdoing. What the victim gives up through forgiveness is the right to revenge.

Do you think these thinkers are right? I'm guessing you do. We would not spend time calling King's actions "forgiveness" if we did not. We also would not contrast anger or hatred with forgiveness if the popular view had no effect on us. There is something intuitively powerful about the idea that forgiveness involves overcoming some negative attitude or emotion.

However, this narrow view of forgiveness cannot explain several important aspects of forgiveness. For instance, if this is all forgiveness involves, how could a person express forgiveness if they never experienced anger at the wrongdoing? The popular view assumes that when we are wronged, we will always experience hard feelings and attitudes of hatred, contempt, and anger. However, in many cases of wrongdoing, particularly with those closest to us, we feel sadness and disappointment, rather than any form of anger. Similarly, if forgiveness always involves giving up anger (or contempt or hatred), how do we explain what is going on when a person reports that they have forgiven a wrongdoer, but their anger (or contempt or hatred) still comes and goes? Is our only option to say they haven't truly forgiven? And how should we describe forgiveness of the deceased when there's no way to extend goodwill or revenge toward them?

Overall, it seems that forgiveness involves more than just the absence and moderation of feelings. While the above stories are typical or even paradigmatic examples of forgiveness, there is more to forgiveness than what has been described. For this reason, versions of the common views of forgiveness are too limited. We need a broader conception of forgiveness.[9] I want to loosen the grip that this common picture of forgiveness has on us by expanding how we think about forgiveness. This is not merely a theoretical matter. As we will see, doing so has consequences for our relationships at home, at work, online, and in the public square.

PUTTING IT ALL INTO PRACTICE

Consider a real-life case of two friends of mine. Let's call them "Ida" and "Jimmy" so as not to reveal their true identities and leave me in need of their forgiveness.

Ida recently discovered that Jimmy, her friend of twelve years, has been gossiping about her. When Ida confronts him, Jimmy admits it and begins to apologize profusely. Ida, some might say, is not an emotional person. She's not easily prone to anger. Nor is she the type of person to hate others. When she discovers Jimmy's transgressions, she doesn't feel anger or hatred toward him. Instead, she feels sad and hurt. Ida thinks about their relationship—the times they've shared, the conversations they've had, the ups and downs they've experienced together. This makes her mourn the relationship. When Jimmy calls her after the transgression, hoping they can patch up their relationship, she refuses to pick up. She even thinks about deleting the photos of them on social media. But Ida knows that dwelling on Jimmy's transgressions will only make her distrustful of others. She also starts to recognize that it's beginning to distract her from enjoying life. After several weeks pass, Jimmy sends Ida the following text message: "Hey. It's been a minute. Just wondering, Are we good?"[10] Ida responds, "Yeah, we're good. But we can't go back to the way things were. Sorry." Ida believes she has forgiven Jimmy.

Is this a case of forgiveness? There is no anger, hate, or contempt to give up. No compassion is extended. Ida doesn't intentionally resist vengeance; she has no desire to act vengefully in the first place. She doesn't utter the words "I forgive you" to Jimmy. And their friendship doesn't pick up where it left off. It seems they will barely be friends at all. Perhaps Ida is just "moving on." But is this forgiveness?

Given how different this case sounds from the stories and philosophical accounts I've just discussed, you have a right to be suspicious. Now, this doesn't mean that you think Ida is a bad person. At least she responded to Jimmy. Her actions just don't look like forgiveness.

I was once doubtful too. But over the years I have expanded my thinking to include cases like Ida's and my own as examples of forgiveness. At first I could not find the words to describe exactly how or why I included them. That's until I came across the work of Alice MacLachlan, whose writing would change my mind and my life forever.

MacLachlan, a philosopher who teaches at York University in Canada, writes about the nature and limits of forgiveness, as well as the role of emotions in repair and reconciliation. I first met MacLachlan when I was a graduate student at what can only be described as a philosophy nerd camp for adults. For a weekend, at a hotel in northern Virginia, we sat around a table with fifteen other scholars discussing the writings of Joseph Butler. Good times! That weekend, MacLachlan, with great generosity, made a commitment to help me in my own writing by sharing her work and by becoming a sounding board for ideas as I completed my graduate work on forgiveness. Little did she know, she was also giving me the language to help me make sense of not only my philosophical view but also my own personal act of forgiveness.

MacLachlan helped me understand that the narrow accounts of forgiveness are mistaken for two reasons additional to those mentioned above. First, they idealize resentment. For example, philosophers often link moral protest to resentment. Getting angry at wrongdoing is a way of protesting against it—it's a way of declaring our disapproval and intolerance of wrongdoing. However, MacLachlan points out, moral protest can also be linked to fear or need. This is not to imply that fear itself is a form of protest in the way that anger is. Rather, it's to say that fear is linked to protest in that it can inform and motivate our protest. For example, I can protest a loss of health insurance, not because I am angry, but because I am afraid of what will happen to me if I get sick. I can morally protest neighbors' un-willingness to wear masks during a global pandemic, not out of resentment, but from a need I have that they do their part to ensure that we can all live to see another day. In other words, resentment is not the only emotional response to wrongdoing, or the only emotion that has a relationship with protest and disapprobation. And if it isn't, then why do we seem to always focus on getting rid of it through forgiveness?

The second, and most important, failing of the narrow view, according to MacLachlan, is that it risks "excluding or undermining the ritualistic and behavioral aspects of forgive-ness." It treats the emotional aspects of forgiveness as if they are the only important ones. There is more to forgiveness than our feelings. There are things we do and ritualistic practices we engage in when we forgive. The anger eradicators' diagno-sis is mistaken: forgiveness can be about how I feel about you *and* how I treat you *and* how I think of you *and* how I deal with myself.

In Ida's case, Ida intentionally switches her focus from Jim-my's deeds to her healthy relationships. Jimmy and Ida engage in a ritualistic practice when he asks, "Are we good?" and she responds, "Yeah, we're good." Instead of looking at forgiveness as a single act (the giving up of certain emotions), MacLachlan suggests that we accept that there is no one paradigm of forgive-ness that is always best. Instead, there is a *variety of ways* to prac-tice forgiveness. And these practices *vary in their aims.*

For this reason, I refer to her account and others like it as *the broad view.*[11] It's an expansive idea of forgiveness that includes ritualistic, behavioral, and emotional aspects. MacLachlan puts it this way: Forgiveness is "a set of interrelated . . . broad and overlapping moral practices for negotiating wrongdoing that may express a number of reparative aims."[12] This is the meaning

of forgiveness. This broad view takes seriously the many practices and aims that are involved when we forgive.

This is not to say that just anything can count as forgiveness.
To understand the broad view, we need to get clearer on the
moral practices and aims of forgiveness. Doing so will allow us
to see why cases like Ida's are instances of forgiveness, and why
our expectations about forgiveness need to undergo a radical
transformation.

First, let's discuss the idea of a practice. Practices are social
and cooperative activities among people that develop over
time. They include rules that must be obeyed in order for us to
qualify as engaging in the practice.[13] For instance, playing basketball is a practice. You must bounce the ball with one hand;
take no more than two steps without bouncing it; and aim to
put it in a net ten feet from the ground. If you follow these (and
other) rules, then you are engaging in the game of basketball. If
you kick a ball with the intention of making it hit duckpins, then
you are not engaging in basketball. Likewise, there are also rules
that must be obeyed for a practice to qualify as forgiveness.
There must be a target of forgiveness, a recipient of forgiveness, and a person who forgives. The target of forgiveness is
wrongdoing. The recipients of forgiveness are wrongdoers who
are held responsible for the deed. And there are people who have
the standing or right to forgive.

If there is no wrongdoing or wrongdoers, there is no reason
to forgive. Consider, for instance, the confusion you feel when
a person says they forgive you but you have done nothing
wrong. You might wonder, "What did I do? But I didn't do anything. So what the hell did they just do?" But even where there
is wrongdoing, not everyone has the right to forgive. Imagine a
stranger forgiving your boss for something wrong that your
boss did to you. She would have no right. So, for an activity to

qualify as forgiveness, we first need targets, recipients, and forgivers.[14]

More importantly, forgiveness also involves broad and overlapping moral practices that are undertaken in order to achieve specific moral aims. This is an important insight because it will help us to see forgiveness where we thought it was absent and to isolate what we find so attractive and useful about forgiveness in the first place. So be patient with me as I pick out some key components of forgiveness to help us better understand that when it comes to forgiveness, it is actions and aims that matter most.

So: back to basketball. I could play basketball several ways. I could play one-on-one, five-on-five, half court, or full court. I could also initiate several moves as I play. I could dunk on my opponent, perform the crossover and the step back, and run different offensive and defensive plays. Similarly, I could forgive by engaging in a variety of acts. They are cognitive, affective, behavioral, performative, and relational in scope. And I can take part in them with several aims in mind, including several different reparative goals. (That is why I describe the view as broad.)

For example, if I wanted to forgive my best friends for their rude behavior, I have several options before me. I could moderate my resentment (affective); refrain from retaliating (behavioral); utter "I forgive you" (performative); come to see my friends in a new light (cognitive); reestablish a new positive relationship (relational); or shake hands with them (ritualistic). Any of these would count as moral practices involved in forgiveness. These practices can also overlap. Managing my anger could help me refrain from revenge. A person needn't do one specific practice, or engage in them all, in order to forgive.

Playing basketball can involve different aims. I could play half court and run different offensive plays with the aim of being the first person to reach 21 points, or with the aim of my team being the first team to win four games out of seven. Regarding the different aims of forgiveness, they are reparative. In this sense, they aim at fixing what was broken, mending what was destroyed, restoring what was lost owing to wrongdoing, and so forth. For example, through the practice of forgiveness I might aim at rebuilding trust, mending my heart, restoring my sense of autonomy and dignity. As we can see, the reparative aims are not restricted to the victim–perpetrator relationship. Forgiveness is also directed at our relationships with our community, our families, and ourselves. We can group the reparative aims of forgiveness into three categories to get a better sense of the goals related to it.

First, forgiveness may aim at *relief*—the removal or reduction of pain for the victim, and moral anguish for the wrongdoer. Second, forgiveness may aim at *release*—freeing victims from the hold that the wrongdoing may have on them. It can also include being released from their own hostile attention, action, and attitudes. For a wrongdoer, it can mean release from being overburdened with a sense of indebtedness or from being a potential victim of retaliation. Third, forgiveness may aim at *reconciliation*—a rejoining of some sort. This may include the fixing of relationships. Although moral practices are broad, they share in these three aims. Now let's put this all together so we can see what forgiveness (its practices and aims) actually looks like in the real world.

I could engage in the practice of refraining from retaliation (behavioral) in order to free the offender from feeling that they must constantly watch their back (release). This would count as an instance of forgiveness. I could tell the offender face-to-face that I forgive her (performative) so that she can begin to stop feeling haunted by the wrongdoing (relief). I could also tell my-

TABLE 1.1. Practices and Aims of Forgiveness

Forgiveness Practice	Likely Aims
Moderate negative emotions	Release for forgiver and relief for offender
View wrongdoer in new light	Relief for offender
Forswear revenge	Relief for offender
Mend relationship but choose not to continue it	Reconciliation
Commit to not bringing up the wrongdoing again	Relief for both offender and forgiver
Refuse to focus on the wrongdoing	Relief for forgiver
Shake hands	Reconciliation
Say "I forgive you"	Release and reconciliation

self, "I forgive you," so as to free myself from a stagnated guilt (release). These too would count as instances of forgiveness.

I could decide to let go of anger or hate (affective) so that I am no longer dominated by negative feelings that affect my health and psychological well-being (relief). Or I could let go of contempt (affective) so that I can begin to look at the offender as a new person and not as their deed (reconciliation). These too would count as forgiveness. And if I refuse to engage in one of the practices, then I would be withholding forgiveness.

Forgiveness, according to the broad view, comprises a variety of practices and aims. In table 1.1, I typify them, laying out a menu of some interrelated options with the three reparative aims.

We tend to think that forgiveness *involves only* the moral practices that deal with emotions. And we think it *aims only* at either release for the victim or a narrow reconciliatory form of repair. Recall what DeVon Franklin realized about forgiving his father: "When I hold onto resentment, I am the one who bears the weight of it." The broad view does not limit forgiveness to one aim or activity. It opens up our options without falling into the trap of calling anything and everything forgiveness.

It is significant to note that the practices above do not *guarantee* forgiveness. Ida might attempt to switch her focus, with the aim of maintaining her ability to trust others, but fail. She might respond to Jimmy's inquiry with "I'm good" and yet Jimmy might not feel relieved of anguish for his having gossiped. Even when there is a high likelihood that the aim can be achieved, this does not mean that it will happen at the precise moment in which Ida engages in the practice. It may take time to complete it. Or it may have to be repeated. Or its completion may require a certain level of support from the community—or a level of participation from the wrongdoer. It's for these reasons that scholars take seriously the concept of *imperfect* forgiveness. Not only does forgiveness occur in imperfect contexts; it often does not go perfectly. Or at least not as perfectly as Lifetime movies will have us believe.

The upshot of accepting the broad view is twofold. First, it shows that forgiveness involves a wide range of actions and attitudes. This allows us to see how inspiring stories, like those about Martin Luther King Jr. and Bethane Middleton-Brown, are instances of forgiveness. But it also allows us to recognize additional real-life stories, like Ida's and my own, as examples of forgiveness too. Forgiveness does not always look the same in all cases. My forgiveness could look like King's in one case, Franklin's in the other, and Ida's the next. This insight can help us see forgiveness where we once thought it was absent.

Second, unlike the narrow view, the broad view gives a more complete explanation as to why we are so fascinated by forgiveness. We are not only interested in what victims feel when they forgive. We are also concerned with what their forgiveness can achieve *and* that it is achieved in a particular way. A wrongdoer may want the victim to engage in an intentional, moral exercise. A family member is likely to want forgiveness to yield some actual real-world results.

EXPANDING OUR EXPECTATIONS

On the narrow view, only my sister has forgiven our stepfather. But the broad view has helped me see that despite my tough exterior, I had also engaged in forgiveness. I had participated in several different practices of forgiveness. I had refrained from bringing up his wrongdoing in conversations with my family over the years. I began to understand that even though his actions showed a disregard for our family, they were also done out of weakness. He was not strong enough to deal with what was happening, so he resorted to infidelity and familial disrespect. This explanation was not an excuse. It was a fact. I also realized that I did not wish death upon him, nor did I create some grand plan to make his life miserable.

I had engaged in these interrelated practices with the aims of repairing my own psychological well-being, and being released from the holds of his wrongdoing. I did not want his infidelity to define, for me, the last moments of my mother's life. She had lived too beautifully for that. I felt no need to dispose of the anger that I continued to feel. I also felt no need to reconcile. And that was okay.

Now, I am not trying to create a definition of forgiveness to convince you that I have the virtue of having forgiven. As we shall see in chapter 2, if I had decided to withhold my forgiveness, that would have been okay too. I am simply suggesting that I, like Ida and many others, intentionally participated in several moral practices with certain aims in mind that are aptly understood as forgiveness. The broad view helped me recognize the long moral journey I had traveled. It also allowed me to see my forgiveness where others, like my sister, overlooked it.

I believe that the broad view of forgiveness will help you, just as it has helped me, recognize the myriad practices we engage to negotiate wrongdoing. There is not just one practice but a variety of daily practices that can count as forgiveness. No one way is more perfect or preferable than the other.

I hope that the broad view *expands* your expectations of what forgiveness can look like and what we can expect from it (and others). But it's also my hope that your expectations of forgiveness will be *improved*. Forgiveness's aims will not be reached immediately. At other times it might not be possible for them to be achieved by the forgiver alone. There are even some aims that forgiveness can't achieve. Recognizing the limits of forgiveness is itself an important aspect of understanding forgiveness.

We should consider these forgiveness practices as advancements that help us negotiate wrongdoing. But, like any kind of technological advancement, they can malfunction—not necessarily because the technology is defective, but because we, its "moral operators," sometimes are. For example, we sometimes put pressure on others to forgive, or unfairly criticize people for withholding forgiveness, and even show disrespect when immediately inquiring about whether a person has forgiven. In doing so, we may be less likely to mend our wounds. Even worse, we may perpetuate harm in the world, even as we aim to do the opposite.

2

FORGIVERS AND WITHHOLDERS

ON AN OCTOBER DAY IN 2018, nine-year-old Jeremiah Harvey, along with his mother and sister, entered a Brooklyn bodega. Dressed in a green and tan school uniform, with a big blue book bag hugging his back, he made his way down the store aisle in search of an afternoon snack. As he passed Teresa Klein, a white woman waiting at the counter, his book bag grazed her backside.[1] Rather than try to figure out what had happened, Klein immediately assumed she had been groped, confronted Jeremiah and his mother, and called the cops. On the 911 call, she can be heard saying, "Her son grabbed my ass." She informed the operator that there were cameras in the store, in case they needed evidence.

A cell phone video of the incident went viral, drawing the ire of the community. Viewers were appalled by Klein's unwillingness to give Jeremiah the benefit of the doubt, even as he cried and held on to his mother, denying the accusation. They were also horrified that she called the cops, given the boy's age and several recent high-profile police shootings of Black boys.

Days later, after Klein had returned to the store and reviewed the surveillance video, she issued an apology to Jeremiah for falsely accusing him of sexual assault. Jeremiah, however, would refuse her apology. At a community meeting held a week later, with tears pouring down his face, Jeremiah told the crowd that "friendship is key." He would add, however, that "I don't forgive this woman, and she needs help."[2]

You might be tempted to dismiss his unforgiving response as immature, a sign of his youth. If friendship is really the key, as Jeremiah claims, then why would he decide not to forgive Klein? But as we will see, there is a lot to learn from his response. Just as there are reasons we forgive, there are also good reasons to withhold forgiveness. In this chapter we will explore *when* and *why* a person might choose to forgive or withhold forgiveness, as well as whether it is fair for us to criticize forgivers and withholders.

CONDITIONS OF FORGIVENESS

Recall that, according to the broad view of forgiveness that I put forward in chapter 1, there is no one way to forgive nor one primary aim of forgiveness. Instead, forgiveness can include a variety of moral practices and reparative aims. Thus, the choice to forgive depends upon the reparative aims that one hopes to achieve through forgiveness, as well as the moral practices in which one is willing to participate. Given the variety of aims and practices of forgiveness, there are no universal conditions that must be met for forgiveness to occur. For instance, one individual, given his particular goals and circumstances, might not need any particular conditions to be met. (Ida might not need Jimmy to apologize in order for her to forgive him, for example.) But another person, in a different relationship, responding to a different wrongdoing, might require that the wrongdoer apologize before she is willing to forgive. These conditions will affect the "when" of forgiveness, as I call it: when it is appropriate for someone to offer forgiveness. And if these conditions aren't met, they may decide it is not time to forgive.

Sometimes these conditions will be related to the moral practice in which a forgiver is going to participate. For example, I may need the wrongdoer to be courageous if forgiveness involves the practice of shaking hands. Other times, conditions will relate to the aims that forgivers want to achieve. If your aim is reconciliation, you may need reassurance from the wrongdoer that they will not repeat the offense. If your aim is to view them in a new light, you may need the wrongdoer to repent.

Now, you might think that there is something deficient with any instance of forgiveness that comes with conditions attached.[3] You would not be alone. Some scholars argue that conditional forgiveness is problematic because certain familiar conditions—such as the requirement that the wrongdoer confess and repent—involve a level of humility and lowness that leaves little room for dignity for the wrongdoer. They also argue that such conditions rely upon the mistaken idea that somehow the pain the wrongdoer suffers through their penitence can atone for the pain they inflicted through their wrongdoing. More generally, they object that forgiveness with conditions is too focused on the past. Forgiveness, in their view, should focus on a constructive future, which can best be achieved (they claim) through unconditional forgiveness.

While these criticisms may apply to certain forgivers and certain instances of forgiveness, they do not apply to everyone who needs certain conditions met before they can forgive. Potential forgivers needn't think confession can atone for anything. They may simply need confession as a sign that trust is possible. Far from being focused on the past, such a condition will determine the kind of future that is possible. In fact, requiring it may be an act of prudence. Wrongdoing leaves victims

hurt and vulnerable. It is wise to want reassurance when deciding to give someone a second chance. One's life (and others')
can depend on it. For example, reconciling with an abusive
friend or spouse before they are committed to change can expose a forgiver to further abuse.

Furthermore, the humility involved in confessing and repent-
ing does not necessarily compromise self-respect. An offender
can show the right amount of humility—expressing remorse,
sympathy, and proper respect for the victim, rather than indig-
nity. And a forgiver needn't *enjoy* such pain or show of lowness.
Indeed, it may even be painful for the forgiver to witness this
display. This is all to say that requiring conditions on forgiveness needn't come from a vengeful or mistaken position. Given
a forgiver's aims, it may be wise to have conditions.

At other times a forgiver's decision about when to forgive
will have nothing to do with what the offender does or doesn't
do. Indeed, a forgiver's reparative aims may be sufficiently *self*-
focused that they refuse to allow the offender to stand in the
way of achieving them. Ida may decide to forgive Jimmy, regardless of whether he apologizes, because she needs psychological
healing. In other cases, a forgiver's aims may be sufficiently
other-focused. For instance, an athlete might decide to forgive
his coaches, even if they falsely deny wrongdoing, because he
believes that withholding forgiveness will cause additional
damage to the team. Because he wants the team to be cohesive,
he extends forgiveness.

In another context, a forgiver may offer unconditional forgiveness as a way to thwart the offender's harmful intentions.
Bethane Middleton-Brown refused to allow Dylann Roof's hate
to win. And so, she forgave. Her forgiveness was a way to beat
Roof at his destructive game. Instead of allowing hate to win,
the families extended love through forgiveness. Some might

even say that they did it with the intention to spark the same response in others, thereby hindering Roof's attempt to spread hate and hasten a race war through his violence.

IN DEFENSE OF FORGIVERS

It may seem strange to suggest that forgivers—as opposed to those who withhold forgiveness—require defense. After all, given the moral aims of forgiveness, why would anyone criticize those who decide to forgive? Shouldn't their noble response to wrongdoing be celebrated by society? There are, however, two popular criticisms that are often leveled against forgivers.

Some are criticized for forgiving too quickly. For instance, we might criticize a friend for forgiving their partner too swiftly by saying, "You took him back already?" We might think that a person who allows their anger at wrongdoing to quickly dissipate is either soft or weak or has failed to appreciate the severity of the injustice at issue. A widespread criticism in the aftermath of the Charleston, South Carolina, bond hearing was that the families offered forgiveness a mere forty-eight hours after the massacre. For some people, this was simply too fast. Philosophers refer to this as *hasty forgiveness*.

Some say that hasty forgiveness compromises self-respect. The thinking goes like this: Anger is a way to protest wrongdoing. And protesting wrongdoing is connected to self-respect. But if you give up the anger (and the protest) at a pace that feels rapid—through forgiveness—you give up the self-respect. The fact that one forgives so quickly shows that you don't *really* respect yourself.

I see three issues with this criticism. First, it equates the giving up of anger with forgiveness. But as we've seen, this is not the only way a person can forgive. This criticism also makes the mistake of exclusively linking moral protest to anger. Recall from chapter 1 that I can morally protest, not out of anger, but out of fear and need. So as long as I'm morally protesting, sans anger, I am still showing self-respect. Anger need not be part of the picture.

But my main issue with this criticism is that, surprisingly, it does not tell us what it is that makes an act of forgiveness "quick." I know that now-retired Jamaican Olympic sprinter Usain Bolt was quick because no other human has ever run 100 meters in 9.58 seconds. And I know that even if you do this in 11.8 seconds, you are still really quick. Just not as quick as Bolt. I do not know, however, what it means to forgive quickly. Nor do I think I am alone in this regard.

Even if we agree that forgiving someone 0.05 seconds after they have wronged you is too soon, our agreement is bound to decrease as we consider more difficult cases. Is it too quick if I forgive someone two weeks after the wrongdoing? How about two months? What's the difference? What if the wrongdoing was a minor transgression? What if the wrongdoer was apologetic immediately after the act? What if I am the sort of person who resolves things efficiently? Should the wrongdoer's relation to me (stranger, friend, or family member) factor into how the speed of my forgiveness is calculated? And who is to decide the appropriate speed at which to forgive?

Unfortunately, there isn't a Forgiveness Olympic Committee to help us settle this matter. I'm skeptical that we can easily judge when a person's forgiveness is quick, particularly when we are bystanders and not the forgivers ourselves. When we lack relevant information (e.g., about the prior relationship between the wrongdoer and victim), we don't know how the victim feels (which is relevant), or we don't know their *aim* in forgiving, it's difficult to assess speed.

Some critics go so far as to claim that when a person engages in hasty forgiveness, they don't really forgive at all. The forgiveness, in their view, is inauthentic. This criticism is also misguided, as it seems to depend on the thought that when a person announces their forgiveness, they have completed it. It is a mistake to think that forgiveness occurs in an instant. Forgiveness is a process. Even when I *decide* to forgive, I still have to engage in the relevant practice of forgiveness. And this may take a while. It may take me years to stop hating the offender, to shake their hand, or to refrain from bringing up the wrongdoing. Moreover, even my participation in the practice doesn't guarantee that I will immediately achieve my aim. So even if a person announces their forgiveness forty-eight hours after the wrongdoing, it doesn't necessarily mean that their forgiveness is complete. It could signal that they are making a commitment to forgive—to start the journey. Their forgiveness has only just begun. While their *commitment* to forgive may be quick, their forgiveness may not be.[4]

Another common criticism of forgivers is that, in certain contexts, a person's forgiveness may send a bad message—a message that forgivers would not typically endorse. The basic idea is that our personal actions have social meanings that outrun our intentions. For instance, a joke could be racist, even if that was not our intention. This is owing to the racialized world we live in—a world in which some words and actions have racial meaning irrespective of what we personally mean by them. In addition, if I cry in public, this might confirm to others the gender stereotype that women are weak and emotional, although I believe no such thing. This applies to forgiveness too. Given the nature of the social world in which we live, a personal act of forgiveness could send a message we do not intend.

A person's forgiveness could communicate that he does not take certain acts of wrongdoing seriously; that he is letting offenders off the hook; or that he even implicitly endorses mistreatment. If the wrongdoing is social and political, this is a particularly salient risk, as the message may extend beyond the victim to others that are similarly situated. For example, a woman who forgives her cheating husband might communicate that women, in general, accept men's womanizing ways. A Black person who forgives a white person for his racist behavior might communicate that whites, in general, should be let off the hook for racial injustice. An employee forgiving his boss for mistreatment might communicate that mistreating workers is not a big deal.

I do not deny that certain bad messages can be communicated through forgiveness. But this is only the first step in the critic's objection to forgiveness. She also must persuade us that these messages are so important that they provide us with a sufficiently weighty reason to refrain from forgiveness. Why should what my forgiveness says to you about women prevent me from forgiving my partner? Why should your interpretation of my forgiveness persuade me not to forgive my stepfather? The critic has to persuade me that these messages should, all things considered, *determine* whether I should forgive or not. I am not convinced that they do.

Why not? Most obviously, the other reasons we have to forgive could outweigh the reason we have to avoid sending a bad message. An employee's forgiveness of his boss may send the signal that he endorses treating workers poorly. But the employee may still decide to forgive because he finds that achieving reconciliation is more valuable than avoiding sending that signal. He need not be naive or blameworthy for doing so. Our own psychological survival will sometimes rightly outweigh what others think about us and our actions. You might be so emotionally spent from focusing on the wrongdoer's actions that you justifiably ignore the risk that your forgiveness might communicate that "you are not a real man" or that "immigrants are subservient." Given the importance of emotional relief, this could be seen not as a selfish act but instead as an act that gives appropriate regard to one's own well-being.

In addition, this criticism is unfair to forgivers.[5] Consider the criticism directed at the family of Botham Jean, an African American man who was killed by Amber Guyger, a white off-duty Dallas police officer, in 2019. The officer entered Botham Jean's apartment, thinking it was her own. Mistaking Jean for an intruder, she shot him. At the officer's sentencing hearing, Botham Jean's brother, Brandt Jean, told the officer that he forgave her. He also gave her a hug. Criticisms of his actions soon followed.

The African American writer Frederick Joseph wrote on Twitter, "I respect forgiveness. But Botham Jean's brother just further bailed Amber Guyger out after the judicial system already did that for her." Joseph continued, "He (Brandt) continued a terrible precedent of Black people not holding white people accountable and that expectation being placed on the community."[6] Joseph's criticism, which is directed at the communicative aspect of Brandt's forgiveness, might be an accurate interpretation of the message that his act will send to the broader community. Nevertheless, this criticism seems problematic. Not only does it fail to consider that Brandt may have had more important reasons to forgive (reasons that have nothing to do with how we understand his forgiveness), but it also puts the responsibility of communication entirely on the forgiver. This seems like an unfair division of labor. Perhaps *we* should try not to interpret Brandt's forgiveness as failing to hold a group responsible. Maybe *we* should resist the inference that because Brandt forgave, others must also follow.

Taking up this latter task, the Civil Rights lawyer Cornell Brooks responded to Brandt's actions: "The danger, however, here, is that the forgiveness of Black folks is used as a permission slip for police brutality, a permission slip for racial profiling and a permission slip for racial disparities." Instead of attacking Brandt's forgiveness, he challenged the interpreters. "I NEVER imagined the capacity of Black folks to forgive would be misused as a benediction for police brutality. I have preached #forgiveness for 25 years, BUT using the willingness of Black people to forgive as an excuse to further victimize Black people is SINFUL."[7] Instead of overburdening Brandt, Brooks challenged interpreters to do their part.

Generalizing from Cornell Brooks's point, perhaps we have an obligation to become more thoughtful interpreters of forgiveness. Perhaps *we* should resist interpreting a woman's forgiveness toward an abusive man as an endorsement of misogyny. Maybe *we* should stop looking at cases of interracial forgiveness as an excuse not to face our own prejudices and biases, or for failing to do the hard work of racial repair. It is unfair to place the burden of making the world less racist and more just entirely on the shoulders of forgivers. We should be careful not to read messages where there are none, or to allow stereotypes and cultural expectations to stand in the way of reparative aims.

I know what you're thinking. So far, I've only discussed what our forgiveness can communicate to bystanders and third parties. But what about the message that forgiveness communicates to the wrongdoer? We want wrongdoers to learn from their actions, so they won't repeat them. And if we are always forgiving, doesn't this send the wrong message to wrongdoers?

I understand the role and importance of tough love. I also acknowledge that, in some cases, withholding forgiveness for a while *may* be good for an offender. But one important lesson of the broad view of forgiveness is that forgiveness is not only about wrongdoers. Forgiveness also aims at release, relief, and reconciliation *for the victim*. Why should victims abandon these goals in order to focus on what the offender learns or doesn't learn? Why must forgivers be both survivors *and* teachers? The decision about whether to forgive should be at the victim's discretion. When we criticize forgivers on this ground, we center wrongdoers and show a lack of concern for victims and their needs.

GIVE ME A REASON TO HOLD BACK

According to the broad view of forgiveness, we forgive as a way to achieve some aim, such as healing or restoration of trust, by participating in some moral practice of forgiveness. To withhold forgiveness, then, is to refuse to participate in the relevant moral practice. But given the valuable ends at which forgiveness aims, why would one decide to withhold forgiveness? Without attempting to offer an exhaustive list of reasons for withholding forgiveness, let's explore three important and common kinds of reasons: timing, external barriers, and self-protection.

One reason a person might withhold forgiveness is that they need more time. They might still be processing the pain or grieving what was taken from them. Recall nine-year-old Jeremiah's withholding. Presented with the opportunity to forgive Klein a mere week after the incident in the bodega, he may have still felt too humiliated or shocked to forgive. In the aftermath of infidelity, a spouse may be too heartbroken to enter the same room as their cheating partner, let alone forgive. Perhaps with more time, the humiliation or hurt will fade, at which point they will be able to forgive.

The psychologist Ian Williamson and his colleagues refer to this sense of time as *unreadiness*, which they define as "undergoing too much emotional turmoil to forgive." As they write, "Since harm of wrongdoing can threaten so many of . . . [our] needs for trust, understanding, belonging, personal control, and self enhancement . . . time is often needed for victims."[8] They argue that how long we experience unreadiness will depend on individual differences. For example, given your past experiences with trauma, you may require more time than me to forgive. Or, given my own tendency to process emotions longer, I may need more time.

But unreadiness is also affected by the severity of the wrongdoing, as well as the offender's history. Even if I process emotions quicker, I may still be less ready to forgive if I am being falsely accused of something as opposed to experiencing exposure at the hands of a gossiping friend. And you may be more ready to forgive if it is the offender's first misdeed instead of part of a long-running pattern.

A withholder may also decide it's *not the time* to forgive. A person may withhold forgiveness because they are *too busy* to think about forgiving or to respond to wrongdoing in the manner in which the practice of forgiveness requires. A family member may withhold forgiveness because they are too busy making funeral arrangements, dealing with life-insurance issues, and trying to figure out how to manage future affairs without their loved ones. An employee may be too busy thinking about how to make ends meet—given their demotion—to think about forgiving their boss. An athlete may be too focused on the immediate goal of winning a championship to address his coaches' horrible actions. I may be too busy writing a book to respond to my colleagues' rude behavior. In such cases, forgiveness may need to take a backseat.

But even when the timing is right, a victim may encounter external barriers to forgiveness. For instance, a person may resist forgiving because they feel they are being pressured or coerced to forgive. Consider how you might react if presented with an unfair ultimatum: "Forgive me or I will tell your secrets." Such an "offer" is likely to make you resist forgiving; and rightly so, because it shows insensitivity and even disrespect. By withholding forgiveness, you refuse to succumb to the pressure.

A person may also withhold forgiveness in order to protect themselves. For example, you might be less inclined to forgive your verbally abusive friend if you sense that they are not really committed to changing how they speak to you. And so, to protect your heart and ears from continual abuse, you withhold forgiveness. Ian Williamson and colleagues refer to this as *self-protective concerns*.

> [These concerns] pertain to victims' qualms about how offenders would receive, interpret, and act on the victims' forgiveness, were it extended to them. The prospect of forgiveness implies greater victim vulnerability, given a diminished ability to control offenders via grudge-bearing or threats of retribution. Additionally, victims may believe that forgiven offenders have the opportunity or motivation to continue to exploit or invalidate those who have extended forgiveness: acting as if the offense didn't occur; minimizing its severity, intentionality, or blameworthiness; continuing to withhold apologies; or repeating similar transgressions.[9]

When potential forgivers have reason to think these threats are highly likely, they are justified in being self-protective. Given their vulnerability, they may decide to withhold forgiveness in order to stay clear of danger. If the offender continues to minimize the wrongdoing, the withholder is unlikely to want to mend the relationship. If the offender continues to withhold an apology, it will be difficult to view the offender in a new light. It might be risky to do so. Lack of confession and apology, as well as denial and gaslighting (by the offender), could indicate danger for the withholder. Withholders may realize that engaging in a moral practice with the offender may cause more harm to their physical or mental well-being than good, or they may realize that the offender is likely to take advantage of them (or the situation) in their vulnerable state. Perhaps this is what Jeremiah was referring to when he said that "this woman needs help." Victims are right to be cautious and thus careful with their forgiveness.

The reasons I've listed are not just reasons to withhold. They are *good* reasons—by which I mean that we are apt to find withholders justified for withholding forgiveness. In contrast to other familiar reasons for withholding forgiveness, such as "to make the offender suffer," these reasons are performed to gain ethical results. And they offer practical ways to escape impending danger. But if withholders often have good reasons for withholding forgiveness, why do we still find ourselves criticizing them?

DEFENDING WITHHOLDERS

Critics of withholders often think that if a person does not participate in the moral practices of forgiveness, then they do not want to achieve the reparative aims of forgiveness. In criticizing a withholder, we might say things like, "You don't *want* to be healed?" "You *want* this to continue to weigh you down?" "I can't believe you *want* what she did to you to take over your life!" This lack of interest in forgiveness often indicates to us that perhaps the withholder enjoys suffering, lacks courage, is selfish, or is resistant to a better future. And we find this unacceptable.

This line of criticism, familiar though it may be, rests upon a logical fallacy. This error is easy to spot once we state the criticism in argument form:

> If you forgive, then you are interested in reaching reparative aims.
>
> You do not forgive.
>
> Therefore, you are not interested in reaching reparative aims.

This may sound convincing. However, this thinking is flawed. The problem with this argument is that the conclusion does not follow from the premises. While the first line claims that those who forgive are interested in reaching reparative aims, it says nothing about those who *do not* forgive. For all the argument says, those who refuse to engage in the practices of forgiveness may *also* be interested in achieving its reparative aims. An example might help illuminate the point.

Consider the following statement: If I listen to Beyoncé (P), then I enjoy music (Q). Sounds good so far. But what if I *do not* listen to Beyoncé (−P)? Does this mean I *do not* enjoy music (−Q)? No! Maybe I do not listen to Beyoncé, but still enjoy music. I listen to John Coltrane, Max Roach, and Herbie Hancock. Therefore, any criticism of my musical taste that takes this structure would be invalid.

In the same way, if we engage in moral practices through forgiveness, then yes, we are interested in reaching reparative aims. This doesn't mean that if we do not engage in the moral practices, we are uninterested in reparative aims. Recall, there could be external barriers that prevent you from engaging in the practices despite your interest in the aims of the practices. Being pressured or fearing impending danger may be good reasons for refraining from pursuing aims that you desire. But there's more.

Engaging in the moral practices is not the only way of reaching the aims. Just as there are more ways to listen to music than by putting on a Beyoncé album, there are more ways to achieve reparative aims than through forgiveness. Instead of seeking relief by forgiving someone who has wronged me—which I may have good reason to do—I may seek relief by pampering myself, venting, or doing some strenuous exercise.[10] When I perform these physical activities—which are different in nature from moral practices—it doesn't mean I am disinterested in repair. To the contrary. I have withheld forgiveness. But I have also found another way to get relief—a way that does not require cooperation from the wrongdoer or negotiating wrongdoing directly.

Similarly, we can also aim to provide relief to those who have wronged us, even if we choose to withhold forgiveness. Instead of offering relief to an offending ex-lover by forgiving them, I may just date someone else. And I may want my ex-lover to know this, so that they know I am no longer thinking of them and can therefore relax. This is not forgiveness. But it still aims to give them some kind of relief.

Speaking of ex-lovers, some animated ones can help explain my point. Pixar's 2017 *Coco* is a captivating and moving story, filled with lessons about family, memory, and dreams. Miguel is an aspiring musician. But his family has forbidden him from pursuing the career because his now-deceased great-great-grandmother, Imelda, forbade music after her husband, Héctor, had forsaken the family for a music career. However, when Miguel visits the underworld and finds his great-great-grandfather, he discovers that he did not leave the family. He was murdered by a greedy, jealous rival. When this information is conveyed to Imelda, it is evident that she remains upset at having been left alone to raise the family. She does not forgive Héctor. "I won't forgive you," she says. "But I will help you." She decides to withhold forgiveness. But she gives him more than relief. Her efforts help him remain remembered by his daughter Coco in the land of the living, and thus he is able to remain alive in the land of the dead.

The mere fact that a person withholds forgiveness does not mean they are not interested in repair or relief. It does not mean they are resistant to a better future. Nor does it mean that they would rather wallow in misery for the rest of their lives. When we criticize withholders on the basis that they lack certain desires or motivations, we are engaging in an erroneous way of thinking. Our criticism doesn't hold up.

Another, milder form of criticism directed at withholders is that, in contrast to those who forgive, they are failing to engage in praiseworthy behavior. We often commend people for their forgiveness, and the media finds it newsworthy to report when someone has forgiven the unforgivable. These forgivers look like "moral superheroes" to us, activating unknown superpowers (aka virtues) in the face of evil. We know that humans do not always respond to wrongdoing in this way, nor do we think they are required to do so. But when a person does, they certainly deserve our praise.

By contrast, there doesn't appear to be much to admire about withholding forgiveness. This is not to say that withholders are blameworthy. They are not doing anything wrong. It's just to say that (at least for these critics) withholders are not doing anything extraordinary to deserve our praise. While the family members in the Charleston courtroom who chose to forgive generated headlines such as "Hate Won't Win," the unforgiving family members in the same courtroom received no such coverage.

Part of this criticism has to do with the idea that it takes a certain degree of virtue to forgive. We think that to forgive, a person must possess excellent character traits. To view the offender in a new light in order to aim for reconciliation requires the courage to overcome the self-protective concerns that can delay forgiveness. Generosity and grace will be helpful in shaking hands on it so that the relationship can be repaired. To put these virtues into practice, despite the difficulty and the pain that often accompany wrongdoing, is something that should be praised. Brandt Jean told a reporter, when reflecting on his decision to forgive the police officer who killed his brother:

> I pretty much . . . hated her. . . . Going through the trial, I just had to hear it [the apology] once, and that's when like my heart kind of opened up. . . . I just, you know, let it all out. . . . Gradually, throughout this year, I worked on myself and I understood that this anger shouldn't be kept inside me.[11]

Not all of us believe we would respond as Brandt Jean did in this situation. His response required putting certain admirable attributes into practice, and many of us are not up to that task. Withholding forgiveness, according to the critics, involves a failure to put into practice these valuable character traits.

Unsurprisingly, I disagree with this criticism of withholders. When I think about nine-year-old Jeremiah Harvey withholding forgiveness, I see courage—the same kind of courage that I witness in Brandt Jean.[12] To announce that you are withholding forgiveness, in a world in which forgiveness is praised, is a courageous act. At the risk of being accused of being bitter and unloving, Jeremiah withholds. It takes courage to focus on one's own needs and pain rather than succumb to pressure from adults and media.

Withholding forgiveness can also display other virtues. When I witness Jeremiah announcing his decision, I see honesty. In a society in which we are quick to keep up appearances, fearing we might come off as too confrontational, Jeremiah is honest about how he feels. I also see him exercising prudence through his decision. He withholds forgiveness because he recognizes that certain conditions are not in place yet for his forgiveness to be beneficial for everyone, including the wrongdoer. When he says, "I do not forgive this woman, she needs help," he also shows concern and decency instead of apathy and uncouthness. He shows courtesy instead of disrespect. He is displaying excellent character traits although he is withholding. This too is praiseworthy.

When you decide to forgive or to withhold forgiveness, I hope you now have a bit of ammunition to stand strong against unfair criticisms regarding your decisions. These considerations will not only help you see through the illogical nature of the criticisms you may hear, but also reduce the shame that you may feel when people—without good reason—criticize you for deciding to extend or withhold forgiveness.

Just as important: I hope this discussion will make you think twice before criticizing the decisions made by others. We can criticize victims in ways that limit their agency when we think we know what's best for them. Instead of standing up for justice or challenging others, our criticisms may get in the way of their reparative aims. By transforming our relationship with forgiveness—and attending to the many reasons people have to forgive and withhold—we will be less inclined to make these mistakes.

3

MAKING A GOOD ASK

JAMES BALDWIN'S *GIOVANNI'S ROOM* is a beautiful yet tragic tale about love, and our fear of and desire to escape love. The protagonist, David, is an American expatriate in Paris who finds himself having feelings not only for his fiancée, Hella, but also a new suitor, Giovanni. As all fictional love triangles go, particularly ones rooted in dishonesty with oneself and others, the lovers hurt each other and the relationships end. David leaves Giovanni for the safety of Hella. And Hella leaves David for the safety of honesty. Giovanni and Hella feel betrayed by David. In recognizing his wrongdoing, David contemplates the question of forgiveness.

On the night when he breaks up with Giovanni, David admits to Giovanni his need to return to his fiancée. "I wanted to beg him to forgive me. But this would have been too great a confession." Out of concern that any yielding in the moment would prevent him from leaving, David refrains from begging for Giovanni's forgiveness—although he wants to utter the words. But this is not a problem in relationship to Hella. David, in recognizing his dishonesty to her, acknowledges to himself, "I want to be forgiven; I want her to forgive me. But I do not know how to state my crime." He wants to ask for forgiveness but doesn't know what to confess, given his fear and shame about his sexuality. When his "crime" is finally revealed—not by David confessing but when he is caught with another love interest by Hella—he does in fact ask for forgiveness: "Hella. Hella. One day, when you're happy, try to forgive me." The reader is not surprised by David's thoughts about forgiveness. He has hurt people. He has hurt himself. Asking for forgiveness is the least he can do, given the circumstances. If he has a moral compass at all, then he would, we expect, ask forgiveness from those whom he has disappointed and hurt.

Literature—from Shakespeare to Baldwin—contains many examples of flawed characters making such requests to those they have harmed. But these asks aren't restricted to the plot lines of literary fiction. We often hear expressions of regret and pleas for forgiveness in our private lives, as well as in the public sphere. We express them privately to our loved ones, to colleagues, and even to strangers we bump into on the street. Politicians and celebrities make these gestures at news conferences, in press releases, on social media. These pleas can take several forms that have subtle differences.[1] For instance, a person might announce, "I want to say to the victims that I am truly sorry. I regret all the pain that I have caused them. I hope they can see just how sincere I really am." In doing so, the speaker is not asking for anything from the victims; he simply wants the victims to understand that he is sorry for the part he played. In other cases, a wrongdoer might make more direct requests for forgiveness while acknowledging her wrongdoing: "I know what I did was wrong. Can you please forgive me?" Or they might say, as David did, "Try to forgive me," after admitting that "whatever I've done to hurt you, I didn't mean to do!"

Often, however, we do not ask *for* forgiveness. Instead we make an inquiry into whether the victim would be willing to forgive—we ask *about* the possibility that the victim will forgive. We may ask on a friend's behalf, "If she were to apologize for what she did, could you find it in your heart to forgive her?" Or we might ask whether the victim thinks she will forgive in the future: "We have tried to make up for all the harm we have caused you and your tribe. Ten years have gone by now. Do you think you will ever forgive us?"

It is not surprising that these expressions often roll off our tongues—for we live in a world full of people who make mistakes and people who intentionally harm others. Expressions of regret and pleas for forgiveness can play an important role in rectifying these harms and repairing our relationships. (On the other hand, being too afraid to utter these expressions, out of fear of what they might reveal about us, is no way to move forward.) But they can also cause significant harm.

If we are to ensure that our requests are more likely to help than harm, we need to think carefully about the different types of requests we make of those we have wronged. This investigation will reveal that requesting forgiveness is not as simple as we sometimes assume and, I hope, will motivate us to proceed with caution when making such requests. Throughout this chapter, I offer a series of practical suggestions for asking for and about forgiveness.

THE RIGHT AND WRONG THINGS TO SAY

Forgiveness requests, as I see them, fall into three categories: commands, inquiries, and pleas. Commands and pleas are examples of requests for forgiveness. Inquiries are examples of requests about forgiveness. As we will see, there are right and wrong ways to say and extend each of these requests.

Commanding

Commanding forgiveness occurs, for example, when a teenager confesses to a caregiver that someone has mistreated them, and the caregiver responds by telling them to "let it go," "get over it," or simply "forgive and forget." The latter response can be heard in the mouth of Shakespeare's King Lear when he says to his youngest daughter, Cordelia: "You must bear with me, pray you now, forget and forgive. I am old and foolish." Another example of commanding is when a spouse tells their partner, "I've apologized. Forgive me already! What more do you want?"

Commanding people to forgive shows a lack of respect for victims by attempting to bend them to our wills—to make our will superior to their own.[2] There is, in general, no moral duty to forgive a wrongdoer, so the decision of whether to forgive should be left up to the victim. It is simply not our place to decide whether or not they should forgive; and when we issue such commands, we attempt to substitute their judgment with our own and fail to respect their agency.

Our judgments can even lead to manipulative guilt-tripping. Relationship experts Gary Chapman and Jennifer Thomas sum it up as follows: "When, as the offender, I [command] to be forgiven, I am like a monarch sitting on a throne, judging the offended person as being guilty of an unforgiving heart. The offended person is hurt and angry over my offense. But I am trying to make her feel guilty for not forgiving me."[3] We should not command victims to forgive—as ways to get them to do what we want them to do, or to feel what we want them to feel. The decision to forgive is theirs to make.

There may, of course, be cases where we will think that we have good reason to believe that the victim should forgive the wrongdoer. Perhaps we think it would be in the victim's interest to forgive. But notice that commands do not appeal to any such reasons. When we command others to forgive, the command gets its force from our presumed authority as requesters (Think: "Forgive because I said so!") rather than from underlying reasons or consequences (Think: "Because it will give you relief.") Victims do not exist for us to boss them around. If a victim decides to forgive, it will be owing to their own reasons and not because we demand that they do.

Suggestion: Never command someone's forgiveness! Ever![4]

Inquiring

The expressions "Do you think you can forgive going forward?" or "Can you find it in your heart to forgive?" are examples of inquiries—requests that seek to understand whether or when a person may be willing to forgive. In the right circumstances, inquiries can lessen or eliminate harm and help victims assert agency. But we also must take care to avoid pressuring victims or prying too aggressively into their inner life. Broadly speaking, there are three types of inquiring requests: *predictive inquiries, introspective inquiries,* and *check-ins.*

Predictive inquiries, which involve asking what a person will do in the future regarding forgiveness, help us understand what is possible going forward. When Royal, the patriarch of Wes Anderson's *The Royal Tenenbaums,* asks his son Chas, "You think you can start forgiving me?," he is making a predictive inquiry. Royal admits that he wants his son's forgiveness more for himself than for Chas, but there is nothing wrong with Royal's question.

Rather than asking victims to hurry up and forgive, predictive inquiries allow victims to guesstimate what they will or will not do in the future. Because this kind of request does not put the victim in the position of making an immediate commitment, it lessens or eliminates the undue social pressure that often accompanies requests about forgiveness. Part of the reason for this is that predictions differ in nature from promises or commitments. If you predict that you will be willing to forgive in the future, but later change your mind, you have not lied. To lie is to assert something you believe to be false; however, in making a prediction about how you will feel or act, you did not do such a thing. You only reported what you thought you would do in the future. When the future arrives, it may turn out that you still find it too difficult to forgive, that you have changed your mind, or that certain conditions have not been met—for instance, the offender has not yet shown remorse or been brought to justice. The predictive request invites an answer from the victim that anticipates these possibilities.

The predictive inquiry can also provide an opportunity for victims to state their own conditions. The question "Do you think you can forgive going forward?" opens up a dialogue in which the victim can say, "Perhaps I can forgive if so and so happens." This is important because we often do not provide victims the opportunity to articulate their needs or explain what they see as possibilities for redress. In some cases, such as legal proceedings, this failure is explained by the fact that we have assigned other people to speak on behalf of victims. In other, interpersonal cases, we simply fail to ask victims. But this type of inquiry can introduce victims' needs into the conversation and give victims a sense of power—a power that wrongdoing and wrongdoers often take from them.

Even though predictive inquiries can play an important role in empowering victims and repairing relationships, we must take care in how we pose such inquiries. Offered in a tone of curiosity, the question "Do you think you can forgive going forward?" is entirely appropriate; however, the same question, put forward with a tone of authority, can be interpreted as a request that commands, blames, or negatively judges the victim.

Suggestion: Ask "What is possible in the future?" But watch your tone!

In addition to asking victims to look to the future, we can also ask them to look within: "Can you find it in your heart to forgive?" This question, which seeks access into the private life of the victim, is what I call an *introspective inquiry*.

Whether such inquiries are appropriate will depend on the nature of the inquiry and the relationship between the requester and victim. When a sister or therapist asks a woman whether she can find it in herself to love again, this question seems perfectly proper. The relationships these individuals share with the woman give them implicit permission to enter their sister's or patient's inner world. But the same question, coming from a stranger, is intrusive—the stranger is asking to gain access to something he does not have the standing or permission to obtain.

This difference helps explain the frustration I felt with several reporters in 2015. That summer, Samuel DuBose was killed by a Cincinnati police officer at a traffic stop. A reporter—not a friend or family member, but a "journalistic" stranger—asked his mother, Audrey, "Can you see in your heart to forgive this police officer?" Earlier that spring a police officer killed Walter Scott. CNN's Anderson Cooper asked Judy Scott, his mother, what she felt "in her heart" and whether she feels "forgiveness." The reporters, given their relationship (or lack thereof) with the families, had no right to ask the victims' families these intimate questions.

You might assume that prefacing the inquiry with "Can I ask you a personal question?" makes an introspective inquiry permissible, no matter what kind of relationship exists between the asker and the person asked. For how can we know which parts the person wants to keep strictly to herself, without asking? Once again, I think the appropriateness of this inquiry will depend on the relationship between the parties. Coming from a family member, colleague, or new friend, this inquiry may be a welcome invitation to deepen our relationship. (Although I must admit that this question—regardless of who asks it— can be vague; for we tend to omit the nature and depth of the "personal" in "personal question.") But coming from a stranger on the street, the mere request to ask a personal question will often cause discomfort.

The social convention that we ought to be reluctant to inquire about strangers' personal lives is important because it "keeps us out of each other's face." But it is also important for our humanity.[5] We do not want to expose every aspect of our inner life to complete strangers. Even if the introspective question does not burden, pressure, or embarrass victims, there should still be certain boundaries to what can be asked of and about us. Part of being human is knowing that not just anyone has access to our inner life and that there are boundaries to what others can know and ask of us—even when it comes to forgiveness. Only those invited by the victim to enter their private lives may ask the introspective inquiry.

Suggestion: It is okay to ask a person to whom you are close what they are feeling or thinking about their forgiveness. But learn to recognize when this may not be any of your business.

The final type of inquiries are *check-ins*: inquiries into how a victim is doing with their forgiveness. We might ask, for instance, "Have you forgiven me yet?" In contrast to predictive inquiries, which ask whether the victim *will* forgive, check-ins ask whether the victim *has* forgiven.

Check-ins are appropriate when they aim for mutual confirmation. Consider the example of Berta, the wife of a génocidaire prisoner, and Aimee, a Rwandan genocide survivor:

> 'Have you forgiven me?' . . . When Berta finally asks the forgiveness question, she is not so much seeking a decision from Aimee, as seeking mutual confirmation of the forgiveness already expressed in Aimee's actions.[6]

Check-ins are appropriate in this context because they are only seeking verbal confirmation of what has already been stated in action. The person making the check-in wants to uncover what has been expressed but not yet verbally articulated.

Check-ins are important because they can help provide clarity about the status of one's relationship. If the offender mistakenly believes that the victim has forgiven him and that the relationship has been restored, his assumption could cause additional injury, as he may cross certain lines that the victim is not yet ready to cross. In doing so, he may disrespect the agency of the potential forgiver and further damage the relationship. Check-ins can be helpful when there is evidence to suggest that the victim has forgiven but the offender remains uncertain.

However, when an offender can be pretty certain that the victim has not forgiven (as there is no evidence to suggest as much) but makes the check-in anyway, it is inappropriate. Inappropriate check-ins can rush victims to forgive, and express the inquirer's impatience and insensitivity. Similarly, check-ins made repetitively, even based on evidence that suggests forgiveness, are inappropriate; they signal the expectation that the victim should have already forgiven, and they can put pressure on the victim to hurry up.

Suggestion: Ask if someone has forgiven you only if there is strong evidence that forgiveness has occurred. Be mindful not to ask in order to rush or pester the victim.

Pleading

Simply put, to make a plea is to ask for forgiveness. Certain kinds of pleas—insistently, repeatedly asking for forgiveness, or emotionally begging for it—are always inappropriate, whether spoken by you or sung by your favorite R&B singer. And they are always inappropriate because such insistent, repetitive pleading tends to rush the victim. These pleas can become a form of moral stalking in which the begging becomes unwanted behavior that brings discomfort to the victim. They can also become emotional blackmail when the wrongdoer proposes to stop begging if only the victim forgives. Of course, all of this is manipulative and intrusive and fails to respect the victim's privacy and agency.

But pleas can also take the form of a *polite invitation* to forgive. In the 1995 movie *Dead Man Walking*, convicted murderer Matthew Poncelet (played by Sean Penn) makes such an invitation. As he utters his last words moments before the State executes him through lethal injection, Poncelet looks at his victims' families and with a trembling voice says: "Mr. Delacroix . . . I don't want to leave this world with any hate in my heart. I ask your forgiveness for what I done. It was a terrible thing I done in taking your son away from you." Poncelet does not wait for a response. Instead, he proceeds to speak to other family members. Poncelet's tone, as well as the context of his request, helps us see his request to Mr. Delacroix as a polite invitation to forgive.

The appropriateness of such invitations will depend on whether certain conditions have been met. For example, one ought to wait an appropriate amount of time before making a request. To take an extreme case, inviting a widow to forgive her murderer the day after the murder is inappropriate. While it is difficult to determine if a victim has forgiven too quickly, for reasons I explored in chapter 2, it is much easier to determine when a request for forgiveness is being offered too quickly. The day after a homicide is a perfect example. When it comes to invitations, conditions matter for determining whether the invites are appropriate. The offender must demonstrate that they have considered the pain they have caused the victim, and the difficulty the victim may have getting over such pain. If this has not been done, the invitation is insensitive and likely to cause further pain. Perhaps most importantly, one must admit and denounce the initial wrongdoing before extending an invitation to forgive. If this is not done, then extending such an invitation is inappropriate, because it asks the victim to do something that they have not been given sufficient moral reasons to do.[7] Poncelet's invitation is appropriate because he satisfies these conditions as he extends his invitation to Mr. Delacroix. He confesses to the crime, shows remorse, and acknowledges the pain he has inflicted.

One reason invitations with unmet conditions are inappropriate is that they are too self-directed—they focus on the needs and wants of the requesting offender, rather than the needs and wants of the victim. In an apology, the wrongdoer brings an offering to the victim and backs away. If forgiveness follows, that is a good thing. If not, bringing the offering was still the right thing to do. However, invitations for forgiveness without conditions having been met are different. The requester does not bring anything to the victim but the request itself.[8] And the requester is likely to expect that the victim will give him an offering: forgiveness. In such cases, an invitation to forgive may aim for superficial repair—a kind of repair that does not address wrongdoing, healing for the victim, or restoration of relationships. Rather, it only provides the appearance of repair, or temporary repair. By offering such an invitation, wrongdoers may be seeking cognitive and emotional relief strictly for themselves, rather than for the victim.

While I have no objection to talking about forgiveness with victims, I do have an objection to overburdening victims. So much is taken from them through wrongdoing. Requesting that victims continue to give—as we remain empty-handed—can overburden them in distinct ways. Out of respect, we should give them apologies, denunciations of wrongdoing, or reparations. What they decide to give us in return is their prerogative. But inviting victims to give us forgiveness, when we give them nothing in return, is to impose additional burdens on them. To be sure, even when all necessary conditions are met, an invitation to forgive may still burden the victim. When convicted murderer Matthew Poncelet says, "I ask your forgiveness for what I done," the parents may have found this quite burdensome. However, because he acknowledged that what he did was wrong, revealed his change in character, and didn't wait for the family members to respond, his invitation was likely to burden them less than would an invitation with unmet conditions.

Invitations to forgive are also inappropriate when they operate as moral tests—as ways of examining victims' moral and political commitments. In certain social contexts an invitation to forgive can be an unfair way to assess whether a person is "really" religious, committed to the cause, or a "moral" person.

Not only is this a bad way to take a person's measure, it is insincere and patronizing.

I've often witnessed such moral tests in public religious settings. A cheating husband, for example, would confess his failures in front of the congregation and then publicly ask his wife to forgive him. I always wondered why this was being done in public rather than in private. But I eventually realized that the public dimension made for a perfect examination room. In that moment, the wife would not only feel on the spot, but she would feel tested—for that was the whole point of the moment. If she did not forgive, witnessing church members were likely to judge her as "not a Christian," because the Bible commands that we forgive others. Moreover, they were likely to consider her a bad wife, and even blame her for the infidelity, because their gender and religious norms dictate that a wife "stick by their man" no matter what.

I discovered that the worry of failing the moral test in the eyes of a community one cares about, and reaping the consequences that would ensue, often informed her and others' "I forgive you" responses. As you can see, a test examiner needn't be the person extending the invitation. It can be witnesses to the invitation. What these moral examinations require are those in a position to judge and social norms from which to make the judgment. I have no doubt that the husband extended the invite in this context to reap results that would fall in his favor. Invitations as moral tests are ways to get reparative results through manipulative and inconsiderate means.

Unfortunately, invitations to forgive can have the effect of a test even when this is not our intention, particularly when they are presented to victims who are often made to prove their morality. Take, for instance, Black men in the United States. Many people often stereotypically perceive Black men as threatening and criminal. We might extend an invitation to forgive to a Black man in ways that make him feel that he must prove how kind and nonviolent he is through forgiveness, even if the same invitation to a white man would have no such effect. Similarly, many people in the West tend to think that women should exhibit feminine, or "ladylike," virtues, such as compassion, empathy, and forgiveness, particularly to men. We might extend to a woman an invitation to forgive in ways that make her feel that she must prove how much of a "lady" she is by acquiescing to this request.

> *Suggestion: Politely invite someone to forgive. But make sure that you have given them reasons first and that you are asking for the right reason.*

> *Bonus suggestion: Don't extend the invitation too quickly. Timing is everything!*

ADDING APOLOGIES TO THE MIX

If your brain hurts from the work it is doing in rethinking forgiveness, it's going to go into overdrive when it discovers that apologies are not without their problems too. It is easy to understand how begging for forgiveness can inappropriately pressure victims. Perhaps more surprising (but hear me out!) is my view that one can place even more pressure on a victim by apologizing before extending an invitation to forgive. The apology may make the victim feel that they must say yes to the request even if they are not yet ready to forgive.

Even though apologies condemn wrongdoing, and we can offer them without intentions of grandstanding, they are also "vice nested in virtue"[9] because they can function to cut off any further criticisms of the wrongdoer. Imagine hearing someone say, "I know I messed up, but I apologized!," as if their apology wipes away any need to continue to condemn their actions. In different contexts, we can use apologies to renounce as well as reinforce power. A rushed, anxious apology may communicate a relinquishment of power, while a slow and loud apology can reinforce power. Apologies can press you for a response. We can also use them to assert a particular narrative, rather than accurately characterize what happened and to whom it happened.[10] The apology can take center stage, overshadowing and obscuring the wrongdoing that prompted it.

One recent example of this involves a Hollywood actor. In 2017 actor Anthony Rapp—in an interview with BuzzFeed—accused actor Kevin Spacey of making a sexual advance at him when he was fourteen years old. (Spacey was twenty-six years old at the time.) In response, Spacey issued the following apology: "I honestly do not remember the encounter. . . . But if I did behave then as he describes, I owe him the sincerest apology for what would have been deeply inappropriate drunken behavior." Note how he claims to not have remembered the incident but then blames it on alcohol. He then goes on to obscure and gain power through it by using the apology to come out as a gay man. "This story has encouraged me to address other things about my life. . . . [I have had] relationships with both men and women. . . . I have loved and had romantic encounters with men throughout my life, and I choose now to live as a gay man." The apology no longer concerns inappropriate behavior committed against a teenage boy. The narrative that is now given is about an actor who has had to hide his sexuality throughout his career but has decided now to be brave and hide no longer. When we use apologies in this way, it's hard to interpret them as sincere, and forgive as a result. More men would follow Rapp in accusing Spacey of sexual harassment and misconduct. Spacey would face several counts of sexual assault in a UK court stemming from incidents that allegedly occurred between 2005 and 2013. At the time of this writing, he is facing seven additional charges of sexual assault that allegedly occurred between 2001 and 2004 in the UK.

Social positions such as gender and race also impact apologies. For example, women—because of gendered expectations—face pressure to accept apologies, particularly by men. Social positions also impact what harms we apologize for.[11] While a government official may apologize for his staff's unethical behavior, the responsibility taken is often narrow and those in power rarely make apologies for systematic practices. All of this does not take away from the importance of good apologies. However, we should remain alert to the fact that not all apologies are created equal. Some apologies are worse than others (and, indeed, worse than not apologizing at all).

To prevent pressure that results when we combine invitations with apologies, the philosopher Zenon Szablowinski suggests that pleas must be preceded by (1) an apology, (2) an acknowledgment of the difficulty of granting forgiveness, and (3) an acknowledgment of the possibility that the offended party may not yet be able to forgive.[12] Without the second and third steps, adding an apology to an invitation to forgive may not always lessen insensitivity and inappropriate pressure.

Although all three of Szablowinski's conditions will give us the things that I've said we should give to victims, I have a better idea. We can meet conditions (2) and (3) by *expressing a hope for forgiveness*, rather than offering an invitation to forgive. In expressing a hope for forgiveness, we articulate a desire for a forgiveness that is not impossible yet not certain either. Unlike an invitation or other requests, expressing hope does not ask anything of the victim. Instead, it expresses a desire but doesn't request that the victim fulfill that desire. Instead of inviting a victim to forgive, we simply say, "I hope you can forgive me."

If predictive inquiries can open up dialogue and provide an opportunity for the victim to present his or her own conditions, then you might assume that invitations can do the same. If a wrongdoer extends an invitation to forgive, the victim could respond by stating what they would need first before they can forgive. I do not doubt that this can occur. However, because of the risks that come along with offering an invitation, it is best to consider expressing a hope for forgiveness instead.

Suggestion: Remember that apologies can reveal moral insight in the wrongdoer and validate victims' emotions. But they can also obscure wrongdoing and place undue pressure on victims. Don't think apologies make everything all right. And get in the habit of expressing a hope for someone's forgiveness rather than asking for forgiveness.

A REFRESHER AND WARNING

It may be difficult at times to keep track of what's appropriate and inappropriate, harmful, and helpful to ask of victims, given all these distinctions. With that in mind, I summarize the take-aways in a checklist in table 3.1 that can serve as a guide. It's a reminder of the options we have when it comes to asking for or about someone's forgiveness. It's also a reminder that not everyone has the standing to ask, that the contexts in which we make requests matter, and that we may need to meet certain conditions before we make our requests.

TABLE 3.1. What to Say, When to Say It, and Why

	Appropriate and Helpful	Inappropriate and Harmful	Who Asks Matters	Context or Conditions Matter	Proceed with Caution
Commands		✓			
Predictive Inquiries	✓				✓
Introspective Inquiries	✓		✓		✓
Check-Ins	✓			✓	✓
(Repetitive) Pleas		✓			
Invitations	✓			✓	✓
Apologies	✓		✓	✓	✓

We should not take our role as requesters lightly. Questions can garner information, but they can also offend. Forgiveness requests can engage victims, but can also deny them agency. Our queries can center forgivers and withholders, but also cover up wrongdoing. Although it is morally appropriate for us to make some requests, this doesn't mean that everything will go perfect when we do. As we shall see in chapters 4 and 5, this is particularly so when we ask for and about the forgiveness of others in public *and* when race is at the forefront.

4

FORGIVENESS AS POLITICAL PROJECT

BETWEEN 1996 AND 1998, the hearings on human rights violations held by the South African Truth and Reconciliation Commission (TRC) were broadcast on live television throughout the world. The TRC had been created to address the political violence for and against apartheid that occurred between 1960 and 1994. I was a teenager at the time and can still vividly recall the scenes that played on my old CRT television. Women wept as they described their experiences of violence and the need to find where their loved ones were buried. I could feel their pain radiating from the screen. Beyond being shocked by the victims' testimonies, I was also inspired by their willingness to forgive and by the compassion of the commissioners in the wake of decades of hate and violence. I was not alone in my reaction.

Almost three decades later, the forgiveness that victims extended and the reconciliatory work (via forgiveness) the committee was able to achieve continue to serve as a touchstone for the possibility of concord in a society marred by injustice and division. Calls by judges and journalists for Black victims of racial violence in America to forgive their attackers, and calls for a reckoning in the United States in the midst of deep political divides—particularly after the storming of the Capitol building on January 6, 2021—differ in important ways from the TRC. But given the success of the Commission in creating a new, post-apartheid South Africa, many think, or at least hope, that America could achieve similar results by emulating the TRC.

There is a lot we can learn about forgiveness from the TRC. The TRC shows us what is necessary for wide-scale forgiveness, but it also makes evident some of the problems with forgiveness as a political project. It shows how *the* model of forgiveness in our time falls far short from the ideal. An examination of the TRC reveals how far we can and must go in improving our societal practices of forgiveness.

THE SOUTH AFRICAN TRC: A BRIEF HISTORY

The TRC is the most prominent, large-scale effort at engaging in political forgiveness in recent years.[1] Created by the TRC Act of 1995, the Commission aimed "to promote national unity and reconciliation in a spirit of understanding which transcends the conflicts and divisions of the past."[2] The Commission believed that only through reconciliation, rather than vengeance, could the nation transition to a post-apartheid, democratic South Africa. Victims were given the opportunity to tell their stories, and offenders were given the chance to tell the truth about the violent acts they committed, in exchange for which they would be granted amnesty.

This work was divided among three committees: the Reparation and Rehabilitation Committee (R&R), which provided support to victims through reparations; the Amnesty Committee (AC), which reviewed amnesty applications;[3] and the Human Rights Violations committee (HRV), which identified victims and investigated whether their human rights had been violated. Local churches throughout South Africa were charged with identifying victims from their region, taking initial statements, and sharing those statements with the HRV committee, so that they could choose who would be allowed to testify at the public hearings. More than 22,000 South Africans submitted statements to the TRC; 1,819 were selected to testify at the public hearings.

Most of the testifiers were Black. A small number of victims were white or Colored—a racial minority in South Africa who have a mix of European and African or Asian ancestry.[4] Victims were ordinary citizens, policemen, and members of political groups. The victims did not testify about apartheid—or even any and all acts of wrongdoing under apartheid. Instead they testified to what were deemed "gross human rights violations" committed by state police, political parties, and anti-apartheid groups.[5]

The HRV, chaired by Anglican archbishop Desmond Tutu—a Black South African native who was the archbishop of Cape Town until 1996—held five to fifteen depositions a day, with most hearings lasting less than an hour.[6] Usually the chair of the committee would open the hearing and introduce the witness, and then a committee member would lead the witness through their testimony.[7] After a sharing of the details, the commissioners ritually asked four questions:

(1) whether the TRC could do something to help the victim; (2) whether the victim would like to know the names of the perpetrators (when applicable—many victims knew fully well who the perpetrators were); (3) whether the victim was politically active at the time; (4) how the victim's life had been transformed by the events.[8]

In running these hearings, the commissioners had to determine how truth would be told and what counted as truth. These decisions, while difficult, paled in comparison to a much more difficult and controversial task: to determine the appropriate link between truth-telling and reconciliation.[9] Not surprisingly— given the religious makeup of the committee, the high Anglican status of its chair, the Ubuntu philosophy (an African ethical system that emphasizes community, equality, and shared humanity), and the Christianity of the majority of South Africans—they concluded that the link would be forgiveness.[10]

Was the Commission's focus on forgiveness the only alternative? Perhaps not. For instance, they could have focused on love or an inclusive form of nationalism. However, reconciliation without forgiveness may have seemed less complete, an insufficient foundation for a post-apartheid future.[11] Given this, reconciliation required a discourse in which forgiveness was requested, encouraged, and praised. During the first six months of the hearings, the committee asked each victim at the end of their testimony whether they had forgiven the perpetrator.[12] Here are a few examples of the ways they talked about forgiveness in the victim hearings.[13]

Mrs. Papu's husband was killed by a rival political group.

REV XUNDU: Thank you, Mr. Chairperson. Ma'am? I heard your story. I only have one question. According to you what can be done so that there can be peace? Is there a conflict between yourself and this other group?

MRS. PAPU: What I want is for them to come forward to tell the truth.

REV XUNDU: You are saying that reconciliation can be built if they can come forward?

MRS. PAPU: Yes, if they can come and tell the truth.

REV. XUNDU: *If they can come forward you will forgive them?*

MRS. PAPU: Yes.

REV. XUNDU: Thank you.[14]

Mrs. Whitfield's husband was killed by an Azanian People's Liberation Army (APLA) bombing in 1993.

MR. SANDI: I may be asking you the same question, but maybe in a different way. I don't seem to get your attitude too clear as to how you would relate to those who perpetrated this gross human rights violation. *Let us suppose the people who did this to your husband and other victims of the tragedy were to come to you and say to you they are asking for forgiveness, how would you respond to such a request?*

MRS. WHITFIELD: I've got no grudge against anybody; I feel if I have, then I cannot call myself a child of God, because if God forgives us, we can forgive others. . . . Here on earth there is no justice. I've never seen justice in this world, but when he comes face to face with the Lord, that is the day he is going to get judged and that is my only hope.

MR. SANDI: Thank you very much.

MRS. WHITFIELD: Thank you, Mr. Chairman.[15]

In both of these cases the committee members asked the victim whether, if certain conditions were met, they would be willing to forgive. By contrast, in other cases, committee members politely invited the victims to forgive:

MS. TSOBILEYO: The comrades and I met with other comrades from KTC, Nyanga East and Crossroads. We marched to [indistinct] complain about the forced removals.

ADV. NTSEBEZA: Now when you say the police shot you, was there anybody who told you that what you were doing is illegal?

MS. TSOBILEYO: Nobody gave us any notice.

ADV. NTSEBEZA: The police just saw a crowd of people and they shot?

MS. TSOBILEYO: Yes. I have several bullets in my body, some are still in my vagina.

CHAIRPERSON: Any other, thank you very much my sister, *please have forgiveness in you.* We hope that you will be healed spiritually and physically. Thank you.[16]

WHAT FORGIVENESS CAN DO

In his book *No Future without Forgiveness*, Bishop Tutu details two benefits of the TRC's use of forgiveness rhetoric. First, he argues that requesting forgiveness served as a direct and explicit means toward reconciliation. For Tutu, asking for forgiveness was a way of "staring truth in the face" and a way to "work out why they [offender and victim] fell out in the first place."[17] That is to say, in their responses to the question whether they would forgive, participants had to make explicit what many of them would otherwise have left unsaid. What human rights violations had occurred, and what was needed to achieve reconciliation, could not be glossed over; participants were forced to strive for actual peace, rather than merely peace in appearance.

Another benefit of these requests is that it made evident the value of forgiveness. As Tutu notes, asking for forgiveness and getting a negative response demonstrated "that forgiveness could not be taken for granted; it was neither cheap nor easy."[18] The request and its refusal showed that forgiveness took work.

The focus on forgiveness has some other desirable features that are worth noting. Beyond the physical harm imposed by rights violations, such victimization also robs people of autonomy.[19] But there's a way in which forgiveness requests can provide victims with opportunities to reassert their power publicly by placing them in the role of decision maker. The choice to forgive can empower victims by allowing them to choose healing, differentiating themselves from the people who attacked them.[20] I believe the TRC did, in fact, provide this kind of empowerment.

By asking victims to forgive, the TRC gave victims the opportunity to exert their autonomy on a public stage.[21] Importantly, both those who decided to forgive, as well as those who refused the request, were given a public space to make or declare their decision; and that act of choosing was empowering. The benefit here has less to do with the value of forgiveness, and more to do with the value of choice: If a society is to heal and continue to coexist after violence, it is not enough that victims and offenders coexist. Victims must regain a sense of personal and civic power over their own lives.

Even without the requests and invitations to forgive, it is likely that some, perhaps many, victims would have forgiven those who had harmed them. Some victims were Christian, and the Christian scriptures encourage forgiveness. These victims might have felt compelled by their religious convictions and might not have needed the committee to encourage them to forgive. However, there is no doubt that the committee was successful in spreading the public message that forgiveness was important for a new South Africa.

Moreover, forgiveness discourse helped open up the possibility for forgiveness. The committee's rhetoric was expressed within a context of truth (facts about the atrocities) and acknowledgment (recognition of those facts). The committee was trying to get at the truth of what occurred. They were also acknowledging the pain and hurt of the victims. It was this truth and acknowledgment that made it more possible for victims to want to forgive.

Sindiswa Mkhonto, a Black South African interviewed by the *Cape Times* in 1996, noted, "I want the TRC to search for truth. You cannot forgive something you don't know."[22] Mkhonto recognized that in order to forgive, a person must have something and someone to forgive. This can only occur by getting at the truth, so truth is a necessary precondition for forgiveness. The forgiveness requests by the committee were successful, in part, because they took place after the victims gave their testimony. More importantly, the same committee that was making the requests was also investigating human rights violations. The committee was also part of a commission whose task was to uncover crimes through confessions made at the concurrent amnesty hearings. Even though the forgiveness requests did not in themselves provide truth, they were made in a context of finding the truth. By working to find something that victims could forgive, the committee opened up the possibility that victims could forgive.

Forgiveness was also made possible by the acknowledgment the requesters gave to victims. Acknowledgment, according to the committee, was an "affirmation that a person's pain is real and worthy of attention . . . thus central to the restoration of the dignity of victims."[23] The committee acknowledged those who were once silenced by recording their testimonies in the public record. They also showed compassion and empathy. In many cases, Bishop Tutu wept with the victims. And when testifiers such as Nomonde Calata—the wife of an activist who was killed by police officers at a roadblock—filled the hearing with a wailing cry, the committee led the audience in a moment of silence or a freedom song. Requests made in this kind of context create conditions for victims to consider forgiveness in the future.[24]

The TRC shows some of the benefits of forgiveness talk as part of a political project of repair. It is an example of how forgiveness discourse can both empower victims and open up the possibility for forgiveness to take place. These benefits are achieved only when requesters truly desire peace, let the silenced speak, extend empathy and compassion, dedicate themselves to seeking truth, and acknowledge victims. It doesn't happen by simply talking about forgiveness—as if it's some magic word. For any community or nation interested in reconciliatory work, they must keep in mind that it's not enough that we encourage and request forgiveness. We must also seek the proper conditions that allow for forgiveness to take place.

A FALSE CHOICE

The TRC's use of forgiveness to accomplish reconciliatory aims was not without criticism.[25] As we shall see, the TRC adopted an oversimplified conception of forgiveness that put undue pressure on victims to forgive and, more generally, failed to treat victims with proper respect. This is perhaps best illustrated by the fact that the Commission presented victims with only two options—a "willingness to forgive" or a "willingness to wreak vengeance."[26] The implication of this choice was that forgiveness should be understood as the alternative to revenge.

It is understandable why TRC commissioners would embrace this view and present these options. During apartheid and before the elections, vengeful violence was rampant in the country. In order for a new South Africa to come into existence, vengeful violence had to come to an end. The way to bring this

about, the Commission reasoned, was through forgiveness—
for on any account of forgiveness, it is reasonable to think that
if you have forgiven, you will no longer have a desire for or participate in revenge.

Even if that reasoning is correct, there was still a problem
with their position. The mere fact that a victim was unwilling
to forgive did not necessarily mean that they were interested
in or willing to enact vengeance. Some victims, uninterested in
both vengeance and forgiveness, just wanted legal prosecution
and punishment. Viewing a desire for prosecution as "revenge"
wrongly conflates justice and revenge. And viewing a desire for
punishment as a form of revenge conceives of punishment in
a narrow, retributive manner. While retribution provides one
justification for punishment, it is not the only reason one
might desire punishment. One might, for instance, desire that
wrongdoers receive punishment as a means to deter future
wrongdoing, or because punishment is part of a rehabilitative
or restorative process. The binary choice presented to the victims thus wrongly attributed a desire for vengeance to those
who possessed no such motive.

The two alternatives also depict anger only in its excessive
form. The desire for revenge is rooted in vindictive rage, and the
Commission's position implied that any expression of anger is
necessarily vindictive. But this need not be the case. The commissioners were wrong in thinking that an unwillingness to give
up all kinds of anger *amounts to* a willingness to wreak vengeance. Perhaps the commissioners understood that anger is
not necessarily about payback but worried that a person who is
angry *may* have a disposition to strike back or may gain satisfac-
tion from the suffering of others. I am sympathetic to such a
concern about anger, as we have good reason to worry about
what others will do when they are angry.

However, not all types of anger lead to vengeance, and the Commission was misled by its exclusive focus on vindictive rage. For example, in the final report of the TRC Bishop Tutu says, "I am exhilarated by the magnanimity of those who should by rights be consumed by bitterness and a lust for revenge; who instead have time after time shown an astonishing magnanimity: a willingness to forgive."[27] In these remarks, anger is conflated with bitterness and a lust for revenge. On Tutu's view, those who have forgiven have given up bitterness and revenge and, because these are features of anger, have given up anger. There is no attention to the possibility of righteous indignation. Nor is there attention given to moderate and appropriate anger. These appropriate forms of anger lack any desire for revenge. The "forgive or wreak vengeance" option presented by the Commission's account of anger presents a false choice; for it is possible to have righteous indignation yet not want to "wreak vengeance."

But there's another problem. When you present victims with this binary choice, you push them to forgive when they may not be ready to do so.[28] If the victim accepts the TRC's framing of their choice—that "giving up of all anger" is the only alternative to vengeance—and the victim doesn't want to seek revenge, the victim may decide to forgive, even if they are not ready to do so. As the philosopher Margaret Walker writes:

> If the possibilities of addressing conflict are represented as "vengeance or forgiveness," victims may feel, or may actually be, pressed to take an undemanding, or even a forgiving stance, even where this frustrates their needs for vindication or forecloses any of the varieties of vindication that might satisfy their needs to have their dignity restored, their suffering acknowledged, or their losses compensated.[29]

According to the broad view of forgiveness, there are better alternatives than the TRC made available. Instead of presenting victims with the options either to forgive or to wreak vengeance, the Commission could have asked whether they were willing to reconcile. If they were, then the victim is left to decide the moral practices (that is, refuse revenge, let go of hatred, and so on) that would lead them to reconcile. They would not be required to abandon their anger. Even if they decide they are not willing to reconcile, forgiveness could still take place—they could engage in moral practices with other aims, such as release or relief. This would be a truer set of alternatives that allows victims to exercise their full agency.

FORCED TO FORGIVE

The false choice presented to the victims wasn't the only source of pressure to forgive. Throughout the process the TRC sought to highlight stories of forgiveness because they believed "that forgiveness would build a new nation from a divided society."[30] The emphasis in the hearings was "the validation of the individual subjective experience of people who had previously been silenced or voiceless."[31] One commissioner told a victim: "Now, please be free. This is not a court of law; it's just a place where you want to come and ventilate your truth."[32] This did not stop the Commission from praising forgiving voices and dismissing or ignoring those who refused. Unfortunately, ignoring and marginalizing those who refused to forgive and praising those who did was a subtle form of coercion that created an inappropriate pressure on victims to forgive. It had the effect of inhibiting forgiveness instead of encouraging it.

In a book based on his extended anthropological fieldwork on the impact of the TRC in African communities in Johannesburg,

Richard Wilson reports that anything that departed from forgiveness was unacceptable in the hearings. The hearings, he
writes,

> were structured in such a way that any expression of a desire
> for revenge by victims would seem out of place. Virtues of
> forgiveness and reconciliation were so loudly and roundly
> applauded that emotions of vengeance, hatred and bitterness
> were rendered unacceptable, an ugly intrusion on a peaceful,
> healing process.[33]

During one amnesty hearing, an attorney began by saying, "It
is time for healing. It is time for forgiveness. It is time for truth.
It is time for confession." When the relatives of the victims
resisted amnesty and refused to forgive, the commissioner assumed that the victims were ignorant of the TRC and its goals.
He asked the family, "Do you read newspapers and watch
TV?" and "Do you believe in reconciliation?"[34] Their refusal,
he implied, meant that the family was opposed to the nation's
goal of reconciliation.

In general, when forgiveness was resisted by those whom the
scholar Annelies Verdoolaege refers to as "non-ideal testifiers,"
they were not only assumed to be ignorant but often dismissed
outright. Consider the following exchange:

MR. BUTHELEZI: I suffered a lot. I almost was affected
    mentally. Even today, I think somehow I am affected
    mentally. So, I am not going to, I am not going to
    reconcile, I am not about to.
MRS. SEROKE: Order please, order.
CHAIRPERSON: Buthelezi, could you, I think you have
    come to the end, could you please take questions.
    Thank you.

MR. BUTHELEZI: No, no, no. No, I have no peace whatsoever and *I will not forgive.* I do not even see why the TRC is existing and how it is helping us in a way. . . .
CHAIRPERSON: Mr. Buthelezi.[35]

The responses of non-ideal testifiers, such as Mr. Buthelezi, may not have supported the forgiveness narrative the TRC wanted to promote, but failing to afford these victims the same respect as those who sought forgiveness does not aid in reconciliation. Ignoring or marginalizing non-ideal testifiers creates mistrust, rather than reconciliation, because it puts the state's needs above the moral and emotional needs of the individuals. As a result, a state may rush its citizens to forgive. New resentments are created when victims feel that their pain is not being acknowledged. This lack of recognition can also undermine dignity and self-respect.[36]

The differential treatment also contributed to victims' feeling inappropriate pressure to forgive. A woman named Kalu admitted the following:

What really makes me angry about the TRC and Tutu is that they are putting pressure on me to forgive. . . . I don't know if I will ever be able to forgive. I carry this ball of anger within me and I don't know where to begin dealing with it. The oppression was bad, but what is much worse, what makes me even angrier is that they are trying to dictate my forgiveness.[37]

Kalu was no outlier. In one study, 30 percent of participants in the TRC felt they were expected or forced to forgive.[38]

When the state demands or coerces citizens to forgive, it reduces forgiveness to a "theatrical gesture on the political stage."[39] If forgiveness is to be something that the victim chooses, then promoting forgiveness in a manipulative way takes away their agency.[40] As the philosopher Alice MacLachlan suggests, this is one reason people often find political applications of forgiveness distasteful: "such a situation offends against the elective character of forgiveness, the particularistic nature of the reasons we have to forgive or not forgive, and also, belies the respect we rightly assume is due to those who have suffered wrongful injury."[41]

While the TRC did not explicitly coerce victims into forgiving—it did not, for instance, threaten them—its expectations and responses to victims who refused to forgive created a subtle yet powerful form of social pressure. Other nations can learn from this. When promoting national reckoning or reconciliation, politicians, community leaders, and the media must be careful to make sure their requests and demands do not create further conflict and harm by disempowering victims. Even when we feel that our community stands in desperate need of radical repair via forgiveness, we must be careful not to rush victims or inappropriately pressure them.

CHRISTIAN EXCLUSIVITY

Beyond excluding those who were not ready to forgive, the TRC's rhetoric of forgiveness also excluded the many non-Christian victims. The hearings themselves were deeply rooted in the Christian tradition, a fact that most commissioners unapologetically endorsed. During the hearings, candles were lit, religious garments were worn, and sessions began and ended in prayer. Tutu not only prayed to the "God of justice" but also often prayed "in Jesus's name."

Although the majority of South Africans are Christian, victims who participated in the hearings included Buddhists, Hindus, Jews, and people of many other faiths. A Muslim victim reported, "On the day of my testimony . . . I spoke critically to an all-Christian panel, headed by an archbishop sitting under a huge crucifix in a church hall."[42] Given the Christian tone of the hearings, it is not surprising that a Christian version of forgiveness was promoted in the hearings. According to such a version, forgiveness is a Christian obligation that involves the overcoming of retributive feelings and attitudes and aims for reconciliation and peace. It's a process that involves the victim, the offender, and God—where the victim relinquishes to God the role of judge and jury. While forgiveness can follow from repentance, repentance needn't be a requirement; the obligation to forgive is unconditional. On this view, the primary reason one ought to forgive is that each person has been forgiven by God, and each person is continually in need of God's forgiveness. Also, there is no limit to the amount of times one should forgive an offender, according to New Testament scriptures.[43]

In a pluralist society it is inappropriate for state actors to invoke an exclusively Christian account of forgiveness. Doing so disrespects other religious traditions; by prioritizing one tradition, the state can force some citizens to accept accounts that are not in line with their own religious beliefs. It can also isolate nonreligious citizens. Marginalizing such persons in the political setting of the TRC implied that those persons were not equal citizens, and that citizenship in the new South Africa was linked to religion. Instead, the state should have endorsed either an ecumenical account of forgiveness, which would encompass accounts of forgiveness from different religious traditions, or a secular account of forgiveness, which would not rely on any religious account of forgiveness. A secular account of forgiveness (like the broad view) is more fitting for a project of reconciliation because it does not require the victims to endorse any particular religious beliefs and commitments. It is an account that can invite all citizens to participate regardless of their religious beliefs.

The religious basis of the hearings was made evident in the TRC's use of Jesus as an exemplar of forgiveness. During the TRC, Tutu often referred to Jesus as an exemplar of unconditional forgiveness, one who was ready to forgive even before wrongdoers asked for it. For Tutu, citizens should extend unilateral forgiveness in order to be Christ-like.

Tutu's approach set perhaps an unrealistically high standard of morality for ordinary victims. But it also seems inapt. As one philosopher puts the point: "After all, there are a number of salient moral and ontological differences between the situation of Christ and that of the human survivor of genocidal violence."[44] Or as another critic writes, "issuing a prayer of forgiveness at the moment of death does not have the same implications as forgiving one's rapist or torturer who may then go on to occupy the same neighborhood and enjoy the same freedoms as the victim."[45] The comparison fails to consider the on-the-ground difficulties and challenges that victims actually face, such as living among perpetrators of genocidal violence.

Rather than use an explicitly religious exemplar of forgiveness, Tutu could have used exemplars such as Martin Luther King Jr. and Gandhi. While one might object that King and Gandhi are themselves religious, I believe that they are better understood as religious individuals who were exemplars for the world. In contrast to religious exemplars, who rely on doctrinal and theological ideas to guide those who accept their doctrine on their religious journey, exemplars for the world rely on universal concepts in order to guide people on their journey with members of society.[46] Alternatively, Tutu could have used entirely secular examples (for instance, examples similar to the family members of the Charleston Nine). It's possible that these examples may not have the same moral pull as traditional religious figures (at least for believers). Nevertheless, they are more humanistic and inclusive examples. They replace the unrealistically high religious norms of the TRC with more realistic standards of what victims' options are and will appeal to citizens from different religious and humanist traditions.

DIFFERENCE MATTERS

As this chapter has illustrated, the TRC is both a good and a bad model for how to go about the work of reckoning and repair. We should adopt the good parts and learn from its failures. While the TRC allows us to identify some of the benefits and pitfalls of political forgiveness, we must not lose sight of the important differences between the context of the TRC and that of the United States. Even if we tried to emulate the TRC's use of forgiveness, there is no reason to expect that we would achieve the same results in our own political context.

In contrast to the TRC, there are no political bodies in the United States encouraging or promoting forgiveness. In addition, the primary issue that the TRC addressed was how its society could survive. This is not what is at issue presently in the United States, as we confront anti-Black racism, police brutality, and other forms of state violence. We should ask quite different things of citizens in the US context. But there is still something we can learn from the TRC: achieving racial and political reconciliation is a political project. It cannot be achieved through media campaigns, self-help books, or private conversations about forgiveness. It will require political resources. Until repair becomes a prioritized political project, talk of forgiveness as *the* solution to our problems—without national commitments to wrestle with history, listen to victims, and rebuild our nation into a more just nation—will ring hollow and ineffective. This is one of the greatest lessons of the TRC: It's not enough to talk about forgiveness. Political institutions must create conditions that can make radical repair possible.

5

WHEN RACE MATTERS

ON FEBRUARY 26, 2012, George Zimmerman, a neighborhood watch volunteer, shot and killed seventeen-year-old Trayvon Martin in what many believed was a case of racial profiling. After the acquittal of Zimmerman, a BBC reporter asked Martin's parents if they could ever find it in themselves to forgive Zimmerman. Sybrina Martin replied, "As Christians we have to forgive. But it's a process, and we are still going through that healing process."[1]

On July 19, 2015, Samuel DuBose, a Black man, was shot in the head by a white police officer in Cincinnati, Ohio. A couple of days after his death, a reporter asked his mother, Audrey DuBose, "You're obviously a person of faith. Do you see it in your heart to forgive this person, this officer, whether he's convicted or not?" She replied, "If he asks for forgiveness, oh yeah. I can forgive anybody. God forgave us."[2]

On July 17, 2014, Eric Garner was killed by New York City police officers after being approached for selling single cigarettes on the street. After the grand jury failed to indict the officers involved, reporters asked his wife, Esaw Garner, "Can the family have it in their heart to accept the officer's apology?" (An officer offered an apology and made it available to media outlets.)

Mrs. Garner responded, "Hell, No! Time for remorse would have been when my husband was yelling to breathe."

As these three cases illustrate, racial violence in the United States is frequently followed by a public request for forgiveness. This is partly explained by the fact that racial harms have a broader sociopolitical impact, and forgiveness is seen as one way to repair the wound that has been inflicted.

Yet, as I argue in this chapter, when requesting goes public, it also often goes horribly wrong. These forgiveness requests represent what I refer to as the *hurry-and-bury ritual*—the public practice of quickly asking victims (particularly women[3] and nonwhites) to forgive in ways that can, implicitly or explicitly, communicate disrespect and obscure wrongdoing. While this ritual can manifest in different contexts, I will focus primarily on examples dealing with race, paying close attention to its familiar appearance in cases of police brutality against Blacks and racial violence in the United States. By clarifying what is morally worrisome about this ritual, we can formulate more appropriate and fruitful questions to ask victims of wrongdoing in public settings.

HURRY AND BURY

There are three features of the hurry-and-bury ritual that can disrespect others and get in the way of repair. The first, quickness, is its most obvious feature. To refer to requests as "quick" may present an immediate worry because "quick" seems subjective. When it comes to our emotional states, what is quick for some may not be quick for others. For instance, I may be able to move on from a relationship within six months, whereas others (for example, my former partner) may judge it as too quick.

I describe forgiveness requests as "quick" if we make them before certain psychological, ritualistic, and legal markers are present. The appropriate *psychological* markers are relative to the makeup of the individual. They are particular markers in the mourning or healing process, such as the lessening or absence of grief or shock.

Ritualistic markers may include such things as the victim's funeral. But these markers based on rituals may also coincide with *moral* markers, such as sincere apologies or reparations from the wrongdoer, and the denouncement of the wrongdoing by others. The presence of these psychological and ritualistic markers is important because they are signs that a person may be more prepared or currently in the process of moving forward from the wrongdoing.

Legal markers, which may include arrests, indictments, or convictions, are often important because they serve as a means of reaching other markers—for through investigations and trials, authorities often make information public that may help the victim move forward. But certain legal markers may also include moral and ritualistic markers. For example, indictments or convictions are public acknowledgments that an injustice has occurred. When Black victims suffer violence from white perpetrators, particularly agents of the state, these legal markers are often absent. Moreover, because Blacks disproportionally suffer hate crimes, they are most frequently put at risk of being solicited for quick requests.

In the cases previously cited, some psychological, ritualistic, and legal markers were not met. A reporter, for example, made a forgiveness request to Trayvon Martin's parents five months after his death and after an apology offered by Zimmerman, but also before the trial and only just after an indictment. A reporter made a forgiveness request in the case of Samuel DuBose before his family buried him. In the case of Philando Castile, a Black man killed by Minnesota police in 2016, a reporter made a forgiveness request only one day after Castile's murder, a day in which the family was surely still grieving and in shock.

Whether or not a forgiveness request is too quick will also depend on the broader patterns of social structure. For instance, in the US context—where there have been recurring acts of police wrongdoing against Blacks and little structural response to such violence—there is good reason to think that requests for forgiveness for acts of police wrongdoing will almost always be too quick. In the presence of ongoing racial injustice, the ritualistic, moral, and legal markers will not be met. However, if these patterns do not exist in another country, and all other markers have been met, a forgiveness request might not be quick, all things considered.

These quick requests to Black victims, no matter what the requester's intentions are, could manifest disrespect by violating what I call the *Too Soon Norm*.[4] The phrase "too soon" is used colloquially as a response to a joke that shouldn't be made, not because it isn't funny but because the event that's the subject of the joke happened too recently. When a joke is made too soon, it can show insensitivity to those who were victims of or indirectly affected by the event. So, it's best that the jokester wait longer to tell the joke. When I refer to the Too Soon Norm, I am pointing to a standard concerning timing. I am not suggesting that we should never ask Black victims to forgive. I am simply noting that, given the tragic weight that accompanies racial violence in our country, one ought to wait longer before making a forgiveness request of a Black victim than one would if the victim were white. This is because the Black victim is experiencing not only an individual harm but also a racialized harm that is part of a broader pattern of harms, and has a special meaning that marks Blacks as inferior and vulnerable. To violate the norm is to minimize the harms by not responding to the Black person with the consideration she deserves. As a result, these requests show race-based disrespect to the victim.

Violation of the Too Soon Norm can suggest several things. It may suggest that the requester does not view the harm as racial or race-motivated. This may, of course, be the result of the requester's ignorance. The requester might not know how prevalent racial violence or discrimination is today or about the disproportionate number of Black people who are murdered by the police annually. However, ignorance, no matter how linked to innocence it is, can still do harm in the world. It can also be a manifestation of disrespect when the ignorant person shows a lack of effort to understand a Black person from her point of view (that is, that they experience racialized harms in ways that other groups do not).

The violation of the norm may also suggest that the harm is racial but not "that bad." For example, a requester might agree that workplace discrimination, racial profiling, and being the target of microaggressions are instances of racial harms. But because the victim did not die, and instead "only" received insults to their dignity or experienced discomfort, the harms are considered not that bad. Since they are not that bad, they are not worth our full consideration. So why wait to ask about forgiveness? This response minimizes racial harms and the feelings associated with them. But it also shows a failure to provide proper consideration to the victim. By doing so, we fail to give serious attention to the sufferings of others. This too is an example of disrespect.

In addition to being disrespectful, requests for forgiveness that arrive too soon can also impede forgiveness and repair, thereby undermining the requester's efforts. If the requester believes that the racial harm that has occurred is minimal in comparison to what the victim has actually experienced, and they refuse to respond with appropriate empathy, a victim may find it hard to forgive. The work of the psychologist Judy Eaton and colleagues helps illuminate this point.

Eaton's research shows that confirming harms, rather than minimizing them, positively influences victims' willingness to forgive. When we as bystanders sincerely tell victims that we understand what has happened to them, the gravity of the situation, and why they feel the way they do, this can lead victims to forgive. As they note in their study, "Forgiveness was significantly higher when the response included acknowledgement than when it did not. . . . [And this is because victims] felt perceptionally validated."[5] When victims felt that others understood their view of what happened, they were more willing to forgive.[6] But even if providing validation and confirmation did not make victims more willing to forgive, it would still be valuable for its own sake.

LOPSIDED AND TOPSY-TURVY

Forgiveness requests in the hurry-and-bury ritual are also lopsided, by which I mean that they typically occur only when certain actors are victims. As the examples at the beginning of this chapter indicate, many such requests occur when victims are Black, and the perpetrators are non-Black or were acting on behalf of a law enforcement agency. In high-profile cases where the victims are white and the perpetrators are Black, the ritual is often missing. For instance, no one ever asked the victims of Chris Dorner's 2013 revenge shooting or Michal Johnson's 2016 shooting of Dallas police officers and civilians if they could find it in their hearts to forgive the Black perpetrators. Nor did reporters ask the family members of Justine Ruszczyk, a white Australian whom a Black Muslim Minneapolis cop, Mohamed Noor, killed after she approached his squad car, if they would ever forgive Mohamed—whether he apologized or not.

However, even if we vowed that we would make forgiveness requests to every victim, regardless of their and the perpetrator's race, sex, or class, the hurry-and-bury ritual would still involve an objectionable asymmetry. The meaning of public requests for forgiveness will depend on who is forgiving and who is receiving forgiveness. Asking about forgiveness in a context in which the victim is Black and the offender is white, and the wrongdoing is fatal violence, has a different meaning than, for example, when the offender and victim are the same race— owing to the racial history, pattern of acts, and asymmetrical oppression and power relations in the United States. Before we delve into these different meanings, let's look at what might motivate these lopsided requests.

Reporters may be more likely to make forgiveness requests to Blacks than to whites as a way of appealing to the agency of Black victims. Once a crime has occurred, the power to prosecute the offender is in the state's hands; and in cases of police brutality, the power to reform internal policies is in the hands of the department. The reporter might understand that there is not much that Black victims can do but forgive. The request might be a reminder of what the victim can actually do, given external forces at work.

The request may also be an appeal to the Christianity of Black victims. Reporters often preface public requests with an acknowledgment of the religious faith of the victims. And victims often announce their forgiveness as a Christian obligation. Empirical evidence shows that Blacks are more religious than

whites, and women are more religious than men.[7] Recognizing
the relationship between Christianity and its emphasis on forgiveness, the requester may be appealing, appropriately, to the
victim's faith. We might take seeing Black victims profess their
religion in public as a reliable sign that it is morally permissible
to make forgiveness requests to them. When the reporter shares
in the victim's religious convictions and their moral framework
more broadly, they may be appealing on behalf of a fellow
Christian. When the reporter does not share the victim's religious convictions, the forgiveness request might be thought of
as a way to respect their beliefs.

Reporters may also make these lopsided requests owing to
the heightened and public stakes of the wrongdoing. Given the
racial nature of the cases, they may remind us that racial injus-
tices are not only historical but very much part of our present;
they may force us to talk about race; they may lead us to inter-
rogate claims of social and institutional progress; and they make
us consider the possibility of civil disorder and disruption if we
fail to make progress. These stakes are not as salient in cases
where there are Black offenders and white victims, or in cases of
white violence enacted on non-Black victims.

However, for the same reason, when Black forgiveness is publicly requested in response to white violence, the request also has
a different significance and meaning. This is the third feature of
the ritual. Recall, those in the hurry-and-bury ritual are motivated by the reparative aims of relief, release, and reconciliation.
However, given the US racial context and the race of the victims
and offenders in these cases, we might want to look more closely
at what, implicitly or explicitly, we are asking to be relieved of or
released from when we make these requests, and for whom we
are seeking release or relief. Many Black Americans, including
myself, already know the answer to these questions.

WHEN THE PAST AND PRESENT SHAPE MEANING

What inferences can Black victims reasonably draw from these forgiveness requests, given the US racial past and present, and the requests' quick, lopsided nature? For many, the answer is that these requests seek relief from white discomfort, release from moral action, and superficial repair.

Black victims can reasonably infer that the hurry-and-bury ritual is implicitly about *relief* of white discomfort. Robin Di-Angelo describes this need to escape racial discomfort as "white fragility" in her book of that title.[8] Whites are often protected from discussing race and therefore develop an expectation for racial comfort. They do not carry the psychic burden of race because they do not often think about it. Race, from their perspective, is thought to "reside in people of color."[9] As a result, whites typically do not develop the psychological stamina to think and talk about race like other racial groups do. When whites are confronted with racial issues, they typically lack the ability to handle the accompanying stress, and they experience painful feelings of guilt. This confrontation violates the racial code that says whites should be comfortable, and this disequilibrium can become intolerable for whites. As a result, many whites will seek to avoid or extricate themselves from the stress-inducing situation.

Seen in this context, the forgiveness request that accompanies the hurry-and-bury ritual is simply a manifestation of the underlying desire to escape this discomfort. The requester may be acting on their own behalf (if they are white) or on behalf of other whites (regardless of the race of the requester). The forgiveness request can be read as a way to escape the racial discomfort that white violence and Black victimhood have introduced. If the victim forgives, we can all move on from the uncomfortable race conversation. (It's called the *hurry-and-bury* ritual for a reason.) White discomfort departs when we introduce forgiveness. Unfortunately, this move ensures that we do not deal with the underlying racism and injustice that gave rise to the wrongdoing.

This kind of request suggests that what is of utmost concern is not the Black victim, but the emotional tranquility of the requester and the white public. The requester has put a premium on his humanity at the expense of the humanity of the Black victim. We can imagine the request being put in more explicit terms: "Make me more comfortable, please! Stop talking about race." But white and state violence, in cases like the ones I raise, cannot be easily separated from discussions about race. Race is embedded in them. The request, which privileges white discomfort over Black pain, is insensitive and disrespectful. The requester is using the Black victim as a means to an end. He is using the victim to make him feel better as a white person under the moral notion of forgiveness. But Blacks are not tools to be used to satisfy our own desires. They, like all humans, should be treated well because they are human.

The inferred meaning manifests disrespect because the requester is showing an indifference to Blacks. The meaning of the request implies that Black victimization at the hands of white violence does not matter, or at least it does not matter as much as white comfort. And to say that Black victimization does not matter is to suggest that Black victims have little or no moral status. But we all have equal moral status as persons. To act as if we do not is to show race-based disrespect.

Requesting forgiveness can also be a way of ducking individual responsibility for making any decision and acting. In response to white violence, the requests may be implicitly asking "not what we can do for them, but what Blacks can do for

us" during this tense political time. To request forgiveness
from the families of Black victims is to leave the responsibility
of responding to white violence to Blacks, particularly Black
women. The request does not ask fellow citizens whether they
have failed to take action to prevent or lessen the problem of
white violence, or what they could do in the future (such as
make institutional or private appeals). The request serves to
reinforce a whole system of race-based labor. The request treats
Blacks as underlings, people who work on behalf of whites.
They are asking victims to do all the work required to make
things better, by forgiving.

While deferring to the actions of Blacks may seem to be a
granting of agency to them, overloading Blacks with burdens
fails to treat them as equals. Instead it reinforces the existing
racial hierarchy. And in the case of Black women, it also reinforces a gender hierarchy. Designating Blacks to take on the
labor required to fix our racial problems is a manifestation of
race-based disrespect that puts Blacks in a no-win situation. If
they accede to the request, then they signal that the problem has
been solved. If they refuse the request to forgive, then attention
often becomes focused on their refusal to help heal the rift in a
racially divided country, instead of on the racial violence that
motivated the request. The request thus says that Blacks—even
when they are victims—are the source of the problem.

Victims can also reasonably infer that forgiveness requests
in the hurry-and-bury ritual are requests for merely superficial
repair. Forgiveness requests often present a misleading picture
of current race relations by depicting racial violence as isolated, rather than as systematic, and racism as a thing of the
past, rather than an ongoing problem. For instance, the newspaper headlines penned in response to the Charleston
massacre—"We Forgive You, Hate Won't Win" and "What It

Takes to Forgive a Killer"—imply that this violent act is an aberration.[10] We've just slipped on the road to racial progress. But we are making progress, aren't we? If white and state violence interrupts the picture that America is beyond its racial past, a nation can view forgiveness requests as the glue that mends the picture. Blacks can therefore infer that requests for forgiveness merely aim to repair the appearance of harmony, rather than address the deeper social problems.

In addition to being disrespectful, these lopsided, superficial requests for forgiveness are also self-defeating—they stand in the way of forgiveness and repair because they are likely to make victims resistant to forgiveness. In a democracy, some citizens will be asked to sacrifice more than others. But as the political theorist Danielle Allen points out in *Talking to Strangers*, the challenge in a democracy is to take turns at sacrifice. Old habits of citizenship entail "assigning to one group all the work of being sovereign, and to another group most of the work of accepting the significant losses that kept the polity stable."[11] Good habits of citizenship entail understanding the need for taking turns at losses as well as gains. A victim may be resistant to lopsided requests because it assigns their group all the work of forgiveness, healing, and reconciliation.

Given the disrespectful messages implied by public requests for forgiveness—that Blacks' interests matter less than whites' interests, that Blacks are solely responsible for healing our country, and that Blacks should conceive acts of violence as isolated, anomalous events—self-respecting victims may be resistant to forgiving. They might reasonably think that by forgiving, they would be endorsing the view that they are inferior. Refusing to forgive may be a way of resisting such claims. If this sounds right, those of us who are tempted to make public requests have reason to do things differently.

USING YOUR WORDS MORE CONSTRUCTIVELY

But why should we be tempted to make any public requests? Part of respecting victims' agency (particularly for victims of high-profile crimes) is publicly opening the lines of communication, allowing their voices and needs to be heard. Public requests help with this endeavor. We will not solve the problems of the hurry-and-bury ritual by simply refraining from asking victims any questions. Instead we need to change the questions we ask publicly (and privately, for that matter).

I want to propose some alternatives to forgiveness requests that can achieve the aims of release for the victim, relief for the offender, and reconciliation for both without disrespecting the victim and possibly blocking forgiveness and radical repair. Given the racial and gendered context in which such requests often arise, we can ask these questions—unlike requests in the hurry-and-bury ritual—quickly and lopsidedly. However, the endpoint of these alternative questions is not forgiveness. Rather, the aim is to make room for agency, achieve repair, and gain an understanding of what we all can do to aid in repair.

Instead of publicly asking victims or their families for forgiveness, let's first ask them: *"What do you want to tell us?"* This seems to be a simple question, but it provides an opportunity for the victim to decide what to tell us about herself or about the victim on behalf of whom she is speaking. She may report that her son was not a monster, that she feels pain, or that this can happen to any Black person in America. She may report what she witnessed. This question allows the person to counter the misleading narratives about race relations that reporters tell in newspapers and that take place in our private conversations following the hurry-and-bury ritual—narratives that, for example, often describe incidents as isolated and America as united. This alternative question aims for the truth. In cases of state and anti-Black violence, the details of what occurred are often unclear, hidden, or delayed. Officers turn off body cameras, eyewitnesses do not come forward, police falsify reports, the media vilify victims, and the "true" intentions of the perpetrator are unknown. The truth is hard to find. The question "What do you want to tell us?" provides an opening for truth by centering the victim's perspective.

Moreover, this question neither romanticizes nor denies victimhood. The question allows victims to be victims; the victim may report her pain, disappointment, and loss without the need to transition to forgiver. Recall that, as the success of the TRC made evident, providing victims with the space to speak and a chance for their stories to be heard can offer release and aid in repair.

Next we can ask the victims, "What can we do for you?" This question provides an opportunity for the victim to explain how her fellow citizens—requesters and bystanders—may help. Rather than place additional burdens on victims, as public requests for forgiveness do, this question doesn't ask victims to do anything. It asks, instead, what victims would have others do for them. The victim could guide the reporters in what kind of story to write or explain how other citizens can join her in protesting and engaging in institutional pressure. Unlike lopsided requests, this second question suggests that we as bystanders have a moral obligation to respond to victims.

The third question we might ask victims is "What do you want to happen?" While the second question asks what we, community members, might do, this third question offers the victim an opportunity to focus on broader social changes. The victim could respond to the question with "I want justice" or "I want body cameras." These are things that only institutions or people in power can bring about. The third question is also an aspirational question. The victim could express future aspirations. She could respond with "I hope we all just get along" or "Please talk about the ways in which we have a systemic problem." The question can provide victims with the opportunity to make political and moral demands. It can also allow them to consider how they might move toward a better, safer, transformative position—not only for themselves but also for other victims and marginalized folks.

Instead of violating the Too Soon Norm and thus minimizing the harm that has occurred, the question "What do you want to happen?" confirms that the event has such a tragic weight that a response from others is needed. Part of responding to victims with care entails asking them the most appropriate ways for us to respond to them, given their preferences and desires. Such a question may, instead of blocking forgiveness, aid in bringing it about by providing incentives for victims to forgive; for if victims' desires are honored, this may give them reasons to forgive.

Although these alternative questions can open up the possibility for forgiveness, that is not their aim. When we ask these questions, we should aim at relief, release, or reconciliation. If the victims are still unwilling to forgive, our questions and responsive actions can help them gain validation and healing. In contrast to the hurry-and-bury ritual, these alternative questions can help us assist with—and get out of the way of— victims' reparative journey. These more constructive and considerate questions can accomplish much more than asking "Can you find it in your heart to forgive?"

6

HOME IMPROVEMENT

ON MARCH 7, 2021, viewers from around the world watched as Oprah Winfrey—in what she later described as the most important interview of her career—sat down with the Duke and Duchess of Sussex, Prince Harry and Meghan Markle, to discuss why they had decided to relocate from the United Kingdom to the United States.

They said they had felt unsupported by the family in the wake of a series of racist attacks in the British media. Meghan admitted to once having suicidal thoughts owing to the press's assaults and the isolation she felt, yet the royals declined to find her help. Harry revealed that a family member had expressed concerns about how dark his firstborn child would be. Both felt neglected and betrayed by their fathers. Harry's father, at the time Prince Charles and now King Charles III, was no longer taking Harry's calls, and Meghan's estranged father had sold his story to the British tabloids. When the two moved to Canada with their newborn son, the royal family cut them off financially and withdrew their security team, which made the couple fearful for their own family's safety.

As Harry and Meghan described these events to Oprah, you could see the pain and hurt in their eyes and hear it in their voices. Their wealth, fame, and (once) royal status set them apart from the average viewer. Yet for many—regardless of class and race—the family drama they described and the hurt they expressed sounded all too familiar. As the interview confirmed, no family is immune from betrayals, neglect, hurt, and conflict.

Family relationships are different from the other relationships in our lives. They are close, intimate, and presumably lifelong. Given this bond and attachment, relatives have stronger reasons to be loyal to one another, to take care of one another, and to avoid doing harm.[1] As the philosopher R. Jay Wallace claims, we have special obligations to people we love. "We have duties to care for our children and our ageing parents . . . that we do not have to people that we do not stand in these relationships with. . . . Duties of loyalty to our life partners that set them apart quite dramatically from the other people we interact with in our lives."[2] These special duties are constitutive of these special relationships. That is, the things that we owe these people—above and beyond what we would owe to any human—are part of what it means for them to be *our* children, parents, or life partners. They give us reasons to perform certain actions (for example, provide support) and hold certain attitudes (for example, express concern) that we do not have a duty to do for others in our lives.

These duties are also, most of us think, particularly weighty. For instance, if I had to decide whether to go to the movies with my co-worker as I promised, or to attend to my nephew at the hospital after a sudden accident, I would go to the hospital. I would not be blameworthy for breaking my promise. Merely stating to my co-worker, "I have to go to the hospital, he's my nephew!" would be enough to explain and justify my actions.

Given the special obligations we owe to our family, when family members fail or refuse to fulfill these duties, the pain of disappointment is often felt more deeply than other wrongs. This can make the process of resolving family conflicts and healing wounds particularly difficult. Perhaps for this reason, family relationships, more than any other type of relationship, often turn to practices of forgiveness as a way to recover from harm and pain, and to mend fractured bonds. Many families, however, are in the grip of the narrow view of forgiveness, and as I'll argue in this chapter, the narrow view stands in the way of achieving these goals, creating more conflict than it solves. We'll see how adopting a broad view of forgiveness can help us respond to and even prevent these conflicts and challenges.

Beyond often holding a narrow view of forgiveness, families make two additional—erroneous, on my view—assumptions. Relatives tend to characterize forgiveness as a loving and selfless act. Families who love each other, the thinking goes, *should* forgive each other. And family members should not forgive to satisfy their own self-interest. Rather, they should forgive for the greater good of the family—or at least that's how the story is told. When a relative's forgiveness fails to fit this idealized picture, it is likely that it will result in further misunderstanding, tension, disagreement, and distance.

MORE FORGIVENESS, MORE PROBLEMS

Let's consider a case in which a person named Mafaz is wronged by a family member, Zakia. Mafaz forgives Zakia by deciding not to pursue revenge with the aim of restoring trust and family peace. However, other family members—influenced by the narrow view—do not think that Mafaz really has forgiven, and therefore they think that she is acting selfishly and without love. They expect her to stop being angry, to let it all go, to reconcile with Zakia, and they expect this to happen quickly, all in the name of love. These unmet expectations in turn create more tension, blame, and confusion, which lead to further infighting and misunderstanding.

Let's take a closer look at what's gone wrong, to help identify the problems that are at the heart of many families' disappointments and condemnation.

THE PROCESS PROBLEM

The first problem, which I'll call the *process problem* can be expressed in the following complaint: "You don't forgive the way I want or expect!" This problem is the result of the belief that how one forgives matters as much as the fact that they forgive.

For instance, when a family member thinks that their relative has not truly forgiven the wrongdoer because their relative has not fully eradicated their anger, they have the process problem. Keep in mind that, for this problem to arise, the relative needn't *behave* angrily toward the family member who has wronged them. Rather, the problem is that they still feel angry—although they have purported to have forgiven. This anger represents (in the family member's mind) bitterness and a lack of love, to say the least. The family member may accuse the forgiver of being unfair by "holding onto it" and may even blame the victim's anger for her own inability to heal, or for the family falling apart.

The process problem doesn't arise simply because there is a misunderstanding about what forgiveness involves. It has more to do with a lack of understanding about the uses and value of anger. As I have discussed previously, anger is an appropriate response to injustice, mistreatment, and harm. It communicates that what we have witnessed is not right. In this way, it expresses a moral judgment.[3] It also communicates value. Recall, when someone harms you, they communicate to you that you do not matter. When you respond with anger, you communicate that you do not accept that message. Therefore, anger communicates not only that we judge something to be wrong, but also that we judge those who have been wronged (including ourselves) to be valuable. Our anger expresses that victims have moral worth and do not deserve to be victims.

When wrongdoing is especially serious, it is fitting for anger to be intense and long-lasting. Even if an offender has offered an apology, or, as in our current case, even if the victim has forgiven the offender, anger may persist. While a forgiver might moderate her anger through forgiveness, the type or degree of wrongdoing, along with its negative impact and effects, might demand that a residue of anger remain.[4]

This residual anger serves several purposes. It reminds us that the wrongdoing is serious—too serious for all traces of anger to disappear. This operates to prevent families from forgetting, justifying, or minimizing wrongdoing. This remnant of anger may also discourage repeated offenses. Pain and discomfort are excellent teachers. When one of the consequences of our harmful actions is the lingering anger of a loved one, we learn quickly. This anger lets offenders know that even if a relative has forgiven them, "they are not totally off the hook." It makes clear that my judgment of your past deeds still stands, as do the wounds.

This kind of anger is compatible with love, not contrary to it. This is because love and anger can have the same aim. Love aims for the best for and in our beloveds. Anger aims for the best in our families and world by recognizing, judging, and preventing wrongdoing.[5] When I am angry, I announce that wrongdoing has occurred and needs to be remedied, and that justice and peace need to be restored.

The anger of a family member can also express familial love. It can express love for the family member who was wronged, by communicating, "I am outraged at what happened to you because you matter to me." It can express love for the family as a group by communicating, "I am outraged at what happened because I care about the well-being of the whole family." Residual anger can even express love for the offending family member, by communicating, "I expect better from you. And I care about your moral development."

I am not saying that it is morally impermissible to forgive by forswearing or letting go of one's anger. It is only to say that forgiveness (and love, care, and concern) can exist where anger remains. In order to resist the process problem and escape the conflicts that follow, we will do well to remember this. We may be tempted to dismiss or condemn anger because its presence generates discomfort, both in ourselves and in those we love. But this discomfort might not, in all cases, outweigh a family's need for anger. My anger at an aunt who mistreated my children may need to remain—for the reasons I mentioned above—despite how uneasy or guilty it makes her feel. Emotions that arise in the aftermath of family pain and drama may not always feel good, yet they often serve important purposes.

THE OUTCOME PROBLEM

Another problem, which is concerned with what forgiveness produces, is what I call the *outcome problem*. It can be expressed in the complaint: "Your forgiveness doesn't result in what I want or expect."

Typically, the thinking is, a person forgives in order to obtain *one* main result—full reconciliation. But recall, there is no one, exclusive goal of forgiveness. We may forgive in order to get relief, release, reconciliation, or some combination of these three reparative aims. Indeed, this is even somewhat misleading, for if we examine each of these individual goals more deeply, as we will in later chapters, we will come to see that there are different types of relief, release, and reconciliation. This opens up our forgiveness goals. It also expands the results that forgiveness can yield.

A family member with an outcome problem is likely to think that because their relative's forgiveness has not resulted in full reconciliation, something has gone wrong. This can fuel disappointment. It can also create additional problems for the family. Families may accuse the forgiving relative of being selfish or petty. In turn, this could lead the forgiving relative—Mafaz, in our example—to feel betrayed or neglected owing to family requests and expectations that she restore the relationship to its former state—to "go back to the way things were," as we sometimes say. This is a narrow view of reconciliation. As with forgiveness itself, there are different types of reconciliation and ways to reconcile.

We can reconcile in the sense of *reuniting*. Reunions don't look the same in all cases. A reunion may take the form of mending that which was broken. My sister and I may be able to go back to the way things were after a minor argument between siblings. But reunions can also take the form of a limited relationship. In this case, mending is occurring, although some broken pieces are left out. I may reunite with my cousin knowing that our relationship cannot, unfortunately, be what it once was. This doesn't mean that the relationship can't be something different. We might remain cordial, even if we are no longer best friends.

We can also reconcile in the sense of *resolving*. Family members can resolve conflict, facilitate mutual understanding, and open up avenues for respect via forgiveness. This doesn't mean relationships stay intact or continue to exist. They might be transformed, or they might need to end. This doesn't mean reconciliation has not taken place.

A perfect illustration of this phenomenon comes from one of my favorite TV shows, *Monk*. Adrian Monk's father, Jack, abandoned the family when Adrian and his brother Ambrose were very young. Instead of confronting his family or divorcing his wife, Jack goes to the store to pick up Chinese food and never returns. Both brothers blame each other for their father's decision to leave. Ambrose still awaited his return. But Adrian did not. Thirty-nine years after abandoning his family, Jack calls Adrian for help after he is arrested for assaulting a police officer. He also asks for Adrian's forgiveness.

While viewers are led to believe that Adrian eventually forgives his father, Jack doesn't appear in any future episodes. Adrian's forgiveness results, not in full reconciliation, but instead in resolution: he now understands why his father left (Jack's own personal failures) and that it wasn't his (Adrian's) fault. Adrian's forgiveness achieved resolution not only with his father but also with his brother. Their constant arguments, in which they blamed each other for their dad leaving, also ended.

Forgiving a family member does not require that we return to the way things were before the wrong. We should not judge the existence or success of family forgiveness by the attainment of full reconciliation. This is magical, Hollywood thinking that has proven to be destructive for many families.

No healthy relationship can exist without trust, and when a relative has betrayed you over and over, it may be impossible to ever trust them again. This is not the forgiver's fault, though. This is the afterlife of wrongdoing. The nature of a transgression can make only *some types* of relationships possible. Moreover, who people are or decide to continue to be can make it impossible to fully reconcile. This leads us to another important aspect of forgiveness.

So far we've discussed what happens when a person forgives a relative for *what they've done*. Things become more complex when we forgive them for *who they are*.[6] For instance, I may forgive my aunt for being the mean person she is. But this will not automatically stop her from being mean. When I forgive her for who she is, my forgiveness is directed, not toward her actions, but toward her as a person. It would involve my letting go of contempt, my feeling that she is worthless, has a low moral status. My forgiveness might come about because she has assumed responsibility, acknowledged her flaws, and taken steps to be better. But self-transformations don't occur in an instant. So, one way, then, to protect my children from her meanness would be to limit her access to them until she fully transforms herself. I might have to decline invitations to her house or carefully navigate family gatherings where she is present. Forgiveness has occurred, but the relationship has changed. I now must navigate it in ways that would not be required if she didn't have her negative character traits.

Family offenses don't just create pain—they often force families to readjust and operate differently. A family's survival may require it. It is understandable that we often desire full reconciliation. But we express naïveté at best, and insensitivity at worst, when we think that such reconciliation *should always* follow forgiveness in the family.

THE PACE PROBLEM

A third common problem, which I refer to as the *pace problem,* concerns *how quickly* a relative forgives. A family member with a pace problem is likely to think that family forgiveness should occur quickly, or at least sooner rather than later. And this is in part because they have not accepted the fact that forgiveness is a process rather than a discrete action. They often, erroneously, think that saying makes it so—that we only need to utter the magic words, and all will be well again. Those with a pace problem are likely to be impatient with a family victim, or to experience what I refer to as *fallout fatigue.*

Fallout fatigue occurs when a person is tired of unresolved conflict and anxious to have it addressed. Unable to handle the ongoing tension, they can become increasingly impatient and desperate. If a victim experiences fallout fatigue, she may forgive too quickly. If a relative of a victim experiences it, they may pressure the victim to hurry up and forgive. Waiting can lead to feelings of uncertainty or uneasiness. And such impatience and fatigue are likely to cause additional conflict.

Those with a pace problem might accuse the aggrieved party of being bitter, petty, and unfair for "holding out." These accusations can create animosity and lead the victim to feel defensive and withdraw from the family. Victims may be hurt by their relative's impatience, thinking it insensitive and uncompassionate. Family members may be hurt by their relatives' pace, thinking it vindictive and inconsiderate. Those with a pace problem are also likely to settle for, or pressure others to engage in, a superficial repair that doesn't adequately deal with the underlying issues.

According to the psychologist and family counselor Paul Coleman, we must be careful about when and how forgiveness is introduced in the wake of a conflict.[7] He notes that if it's introduced prematurely, the victim may rebel because it places the burden of resolving conflict on their shoulders. He acknowledges that he introduces the topic only once progress has been made in the sessions—that is, when some level of trust has been restored and communication has been improved. And he cautions therapy practitioners not to discuss forgiveness immediately. We can apply his professional advice to our interpersonal worlds.

It is easy to understand why, in the aftermath of family conflict, many rush to talk about forgiveness or expect the party who has been wronged to quickly extend it. Family is important for many of us. Our hearts break over threats that our families could fall apart. However, regardless of our good intentions, this impatience for forgiveness has significant problems, akin to the problems presented by the "hurry-and-bury ritual" I discussed in chapter 5. Quickly asking and expecting forgiveness from those we love can disrespect and endanger them. We should, instead, put in practice the *wait-and-relate principle*.

This principle involves *waiting* for our loved ones to forgive, refusing to put them on our own forgiveness schedule. The fact that I have forgiven a hitherto beloved auntie for a transgression doesn't mean that my siblings or cousins should do so at the same pace. Waiting is about communicating to our relatives that the decision to travel the road to forgiveness, as well as the pace of their journey, is up to them. When we wait, we acknowledge and respect the fact that everyone has their own process, and that each person will experience the wrongdoing in different ways. Given this diversity of experience, some will naturally take longer than others to forgive or want to forgive.

To understand what we should and shouldn't do while we wait, let's consider an analogy. Think about the last marathon you watched (assuming you have the patience to do such a thing). You may have noticed runners leading a pack and then dropping out after some distance. Those runners are known as pacemakers or "rabbits." They help runners stay at a speed that they can manage for the twenty-six miles of the race. And they know this speed because they have trained with members of the pack. Their job is not to win the race. It's to set a pace with the hopes that team members finish at their personal best.

The same role applies to us as family members. We should do our best to help our loved ones—on the long road to forgiveness—get there at a pace that *they* (not we) can manage. And we might have some clue concerning that pace because we have talked with them, empathized with them, and know their strengths, weaknesses, and difficulties. But our job is not to rush our relatives to forgive, nor is it to beat them to forgiveness as if it's a competition. Our job is to help them do their best. We can help them do it at their pace, but then, like Kenyan runner Eliud Kipchoge's rabbits did when he completed a record marathon in under two hours, it's best for us to get out of the way and let them do the rest.

This is a form of waiting, but far from being passive, it is *active waiting*. As we wait, we are not doing nothing. Instead, we cautiously and lovingly do what we can to help open up the possibilities for their forgiveness by, for instance, reiterating that what happened to them was not OK, listening to their struggles, extending kindness, and offering support.

Relating is about showing concern and compassion. It's about trying to understand the pain and difficulties of those who can't forgive as soon as we think they should. Often, relating makes it easier to wait. For example, as Coleman notes, if you discover that the intensity of a spouse's anger toward you for some transgression is explained, in part, by their mother or father often having done the thing you have done, this can help you understand why forgiveness is taking longer than it reasonably would. Relating will help you see that perhaps they need to forgive their parents first before they can forgive you, which may make it easier to wait for forgiveness.

At other times, waiting will help you to relate. As you wait for forgiveness, certain things may reveal themselves to you. You might be reminded of how you have been hurt by others in the past and that it took you some time to get through it and forgive. If it happened to you, then you can be patient when the shoe is on the other foot. You might begin to realize how insensitive or selfish you are being in expecting quick forgiveness and then decide to do better as a result. The time you take to reflect can lead to empathy, and empathy can lead to relating better.

A variety of things go by the name "empathy." The philosopher Samuel Fleischacker distinguishes two main camps: contagious empathy and projective empathy. We typically think that empathy involves feeling or sharing in the emotions of others (contagion) or imagining ourselves in the situations of others (projection). I am apt to think that projective empathy is more helpful than contagious empathy when it comes to relating. Simply "catching" the sadness of my loved ones will not help me relate to them better. I can catch sadness by simply witnessing my stepbrother's tears without knowing anything about what caused his sadness. But such knowledge and understanding is important to relating to him. Projective empathy requires me to know *why* he is sad. As Fleischacker writes, "[projective empathy] requires us to attend to the entire character and perspective of the other person, rather than just her momentary experiences."[8] It requires not merely that we listen to the other person, but that we "ask the questions whose answers need to be listened to. Empathy requires inquiry as much as imagination."[9] When we ask questions, listen to answers, aim to know the person and the full circumstances (that is, when we are empathizing), we are able to relate more to our hurting relatives. Empathy thus plays an important role in the wait-and-relate cycle.

When we are impatient, tired of being reminded of our past, or feel ourselves getting resentful about our relatives' persistent resentment, we should remind ourselves to wait and relate. Waiting and relating might not get us the instant gratification we think we desperately need. But in this case the adage is true—good things do come to those who wait.

THE PROTECTION PROBLEM

Finally, the *protection problem* is concerned with making sure that forgiveness protects certain family members or the family's reputation in ways that can obscure wrongdoing and expose victims to future harms. It can be expressed in the complaint: "You should forgive for the sake of the children" or "You should forgive to preserve the family name."

In the family, those with a protection problem purport to aim for the greater good. They are concerned with what philosophers refer to as "prudential considerations."[10] These considerations focus on the positive goods that forgiveness can achieve (such as making Thanksgiving dinners more tolerable). This is a prudential consideration. The problem occurs, however, when the greater good turns out not to be good at all.

The greater good achieved by forgiveness can refer to a variety of things. It could mean, for instance, the number of people who are positively affected by forgiveness; the protection of a valuable or powerful family member; or the shielding of the family's public reputation. Family members may want or expect their relatives to forgive, not for the relative's own individual good, but in the interests of other family members. We may hear a grandmother tell her granddaughter to forgive her husband for the sake of the children. She is asking the mother to protect the kids from the possibility of being raised by a single parent. Or an older brother may want or expect his younger brother to forgive his molesting yet powerful uncle, so that the uncle will not face criminal charges. Or so that his crimes will not be publicly revealed, which would bring shame on the whole family.

But the protection problem doesn't protect everyone. It protects the children but not the mother; the uncle but not the brother; the family's reputation but not vulnerable children. While the children might be protected from being fatherless, the mother will continue to be exposed to physical violence. While the good family name stays intact, family trauma and violation are shielded and persist. The protection problem tends to risk the safety of the most vulnerable family members: women and children. When we view forgiveness as the *only* available response to malicious and unlawful behavior in our families, or as a way to obscure wrongful behavior, no one will ever be safe.

The protection problem, to my mind, is the most egregious of family problems concerning forgiveness, as it involves significant corruption of family relationships. Family members who have a protection problem are likely to condone wrongdoing in the name of forgiveness. This occurs when they use a relative's forgiveness as a permission slip to tolerate abusive behavior. When we protect abusive members or our family's reputation in this way, the victim might continue to suffer violations, abuse, and even death.

We also make ourselves complicit in wrongful, unlawful behavior. As the sociologist and peace activist Joseph Elder writes: "Interpersonal forgiveness is *not* accepting or tolerating injustice . . . *nor* is it forgetting, condoning, or excusing wrongdoing . . . or granting a legal pardon."[11] Just as the family members of the Charleston Nine forgave Dylann Roof *and* demanded justice, our own families can forgive each other *and* demand consequences. When we equate forgiveness with tolerating or excusing misconduct, we breed more trauma, which is antithetical to the basic idea that families should provide security to one another.

While there are different opinions as to what constitutes a family, as well as different types and kinds of families, there is one thing we think families (should) share in common. We expect family members to extend care. More than any other institution, family members are expected to care about and for each other, as well as provide and receive care.[12] That is to say, we expect that families will recognize when a relative is in need of care, take responsibility for meeting that need, and engage in the actual work of providing it. When a family fails to do so, we are all likely to think that something is out of order, missing, heartbreaking, or flat-out wrong. This is precisely how I felt as I watched Yasujirō Ozu's 1953 groundbreaking film *Tokyo Story* for the first time.

In addition to being a visual masterpiece, the film provides an emotionally powerful portrait of a family's relations and the family's changing nature. When two elderly parents visit their adult children in the big city, the children treat them, not as revered guests, but as inconveniences. Even the grandchildren are indifferent to their visit. When one of the daughter's customers asks who they are, the daughter does not even acknowledge that they are her parents—she tells the customer that they are friends from the country. As the elderly parents begin their journey home, the matriarch gets sick on the train. They decide to get off at the closest station, near where their son lives. The son later describes his mother's sickness to a colleague as a "real bother" for him.

There is a lack of care extended to the parents. But they don't complain or verbally express their hurt. Nevertheless, you (as a viewer) can see and feel the parents' heartbreak and disappointment, and the distance that is unacknowledged yet real indeed. At the same time, you are challenged to be better extenders of care in your own family, to be careful that you don't repeat these children's mistakes. In essence, as Ozu exposes us to a tragic image of a lack of care, he challenges us to be ever conscious of the need for care within the family.

The emotional distance conveyed in the film strikes us because it is at odds with our understanding of the family as the paradigmatic example of care relations. When families adopt the protective problem, though, they are choosing complicity and reputation at the expense of care.

This is not to say that it is impossible to care in the wrong ways or for the wrong things. A grandmother may think that she is caring about and for her grandchildren when she advises the mother to protect the kids by forgiving her spouse. In this case, the best way to escape the protective problem is to refrain from paternalist thinking whereby we believe that we know what's best for our loved ones. We can provide better care by listening to victims and decentering ourselves. These are pathways to authentic familial protection and care—not the faux selective kind that obscures conflict and creates long-lasting trauma.

Table 6.1 presents a summary of family problems around forgiveness, along with their associated complaints, motivating feelings and attitudes, additional conflicts they create, and some possible solutions:

TABLE 6.1. Tackling the Problem

Problem	Complaint	Feelings/Attitudes Driving It	Conflicts and Harms	Some Solutions
Process Problem	You don't forgive the way I want you to!	Guilt, uncertainty, fear	Victim-blaming	Make room for anger
Outcome Problem	Your forgiveness doesn't result in what I want!	Disappointment, romanticism, selfishness	Neglect and unfair pressure	Expand your forgiveness goals
Pace Problem	You don't forgive as quick as I want you to!	Anxiety, impatience, desperation, fallout fatigue	Insensitivity and settling	Wait and relate
Protection Problem	Forgive for the sake of others!	Fear, shame, and lack of compassion	Downplaying abuse, condoning, and increased vulnerability	Care, listen, and decenter

IT'S A FAMILY AFFAIR

If you were to go on national television to discuss your family's problems with someone like Oprah Winfrey, I'm sure you could share events and disappointments that would make audiences weep. And there are lots of details that you might omit, too, for fear of appearing petty. All of us have experienced hurt at the hands of our family, and we have almost certainly caused pain ourselves. Many of us turn to forgiveness as a possible antidote. But forgiveness, like any powerful medicine, works only if it is applied properly. If we are reckless and imposing, our rush toward forgiveness can deepen wounds, which will fester long after the initial wrong. Often we impose our own views about forgiveness—how and when it should occur, what it should aim to achieve—not because we don't care, but because we either care for the wrong things and the wrong people, or care in the wrong way. But we are not doomed to failure. Once we understand the problems that our expectations for forgiveness are motivated by, we can begin to do better.

7

THE BUSINESS OF FORGIVENESS

DUNDER MIFFLIN is a fictitious paper supply company whose day-to-day operations are depicted in *The Office*—a mockumentary series that ran for nine seasons on NBC. With the aim of providing "Limitless Paper in a Paperless World," its Scranton branch employees, led by manager Michael Scott, come to work each day to sell and innovate. This work requires collaboration, of course. However, interoffice conflict disrupts employees' well-being and the teamwork required for the business to succeed.

Phyllis is constantly the butt of her manager's jokes. Ryan talks behind his co-worker's back. Angela calls social services on Pam for drinking soda while pregnant and calls Immigration Services on Oscar for being "Mexican American." Dwight once sent a misogynistic memo to employees, recommending that women not speak to strangers without his consent and that there be restrictions on their clothing. The worst offender, of course, is Michael, who is happy to gossip about his colleagues' affairs, outs his gay co-worker, and occasionally fires people as a practical joke.

The Office was popular with fans not only because its dialogue was hilarious and memorable but also because its depiction of white-collar office conflict (initiated by weirdos, sweethearts, and bullies) was so relatable. Petty, inappropriate, childish, insensitive, aggressive, and patronizing behavior can create conflict at any workplace. But how do you properly respond? Is forgiveness the cure?

If we were sitcom screenwriters and had to give a name to an episode of a current real-life corporate solution, we could call it "Forgiveness Week," because it's become faddish for organizations to create a "culture of forgiveness" to respond to workplace conflict.

Indeed, in business and management schools across the United States, future leaders are studying forgiveness. More than 150,000 articles have been written about forgiveness in organizations in the last decade alone. Articles in mainstream publications targeting entrepreneurs argue that you should forgive your work nemesis;[1] link forgiveness to business leaders' comebacks after errors and even scandals;[2] and suggest ways to achieve brand forgiveness.[3] Forgiveness, it seems, is a best business practice.

In this chapter I caution against overselling forgiveness in the workplace. Instead we should focus more on creating a work environment that's active in curbing conflict. But because conflicts will arise, I recommend ways to resolve and recover from wrongdoing without condoning it or overburdening employees. I'll suggest that businesses should focus their energies on creating a climate that's ripe for forgiveness rather than pushing employees to forgive.

FORGIVENESS AS THE SECRET TO SUCCESS?

You don't have to watch an episode of *The Office* to know that conflict at work is linked to stress, health problems, and hostility. You probably have lots of firsthand evidence at your disposal to prove it. Conflict can also distract from productivity and reduce cooperation. Yet conflict itself is inevitable and not necessarily the central problem—rather, it is *how we respond* to conflict that predicts whether things like tension and anxiety will persist.

One response that has received significant attention in conflict-resolution literature is forgiveness. The management specialist Michael Stone claims that a lack of forgiveness, in the aftermath of conflict, has a negative impact on multiple levels of an organization. On the individual level, it can create alienation, withdrawal, unhappiness, and lack of creativity. On the team level, it can create distance, negative politics, and lack of common direction. And on the organizational level, it can produce mistrust, low allegiance, and high turnover.[4]

Forgiveness, on the contrary, is believed to break the conflict cycle and contribute to employee retention, helping behavior, and interpersonal citizenship behavior.[5] Again, these contributions occur at multiple levels of the organization. On the individual level, forgiveness can create happiness, vibrant health, peace of mind, and creativity. On the team level, forgiveness can create interconnection, the feeling of community, and mutual support. On the organizational level, it can make work feel meaningful, improve employee retention, and generate an overall focus on service.[6]

Social psychologists who have sought to put these claims to the test have found that there is at least some association between forgiveness and well-being in the workplace. In one study consisting of participants from a variety of career fields, researchers found that forgiveness is linked to fewer physical and mental health problems associated with workplace conflict. Participants who reported to have forgiven a workplace offense also reported an increase in work productivity.[7] This led researchers to conclude that "reducing unforgiveness and promoting forgiveness may be promising and fruitful avenues to optimizing workplace relationships, well-being, productive performance, and related savings and profitability."[8]

In other words, if a healthy workplace is vital to employees' well-being and positive work outcomes, and forgiveness is linked to such outcomes, then forgiveness is important and should be promoted. Forgiveness, it seems at first blush, counteracts the bad effects of conflict and inspires positive outcomes.

However, these results only point to associations. The fact that positive outcomes are linked to forgiveness does not mean that promoting forgiveness would help. Correlation isn't causation. So psychologists set out to see what happens if forgiveness is promoted in the workplace. Could such training result in improvements in employees' productivity and well-being in the aftermath of conflict?

To test this, researchers designed a pilot program to measure the effect of forgiveness on sales and well-being after participants underwent forgiveness training—the first-ever attempt to teach forgiveness to employees.[9] The program, which took place over a period of six to twelve months, consisted of 104 participants from the financial services industry, who were divided into six cohorts. For the project, researchers defined forgiveness as "the releasing of negative emotions and the extending of positive emotions, attitudes, and behavior towards the wrongdoer."[10]

The first part of the training attempted to instill in participants the idea that forgiveness is a key aspect and enhancement of emotional intelligence—a broad family of skills (self-awareness, self-regulation, empathy, social skills, and motivation) thought to make great leaders and help workers be effective. The other half of the training focused on techniques for stress management and taught participants to practice the nine steps to forgiveness, which included knowing exactly how you feel about what happened, amending your grievance story, and remembering that a life well lived is your best revenge.[11] Participants were also provided with individual plans and coaches to help them tackle their forgiveness-related weaknesses.

At the end of the study, participants who completed the program were assessed with respect to productivity, stress, anger, positive states, health-related quality of life, and physical vitality. The researchers found that, compared to the control group, the training resulted in several positive outcomes. For example, participants experienced decreases in stress (by 23 percent) and anger (by 13 percent), as well as increases in positive states (by 20 percent) and quality of life (by 10 percent).[12] The researchers concluded that teaching employees forgiveness skills *proactively*—before conflict arises—can promote wellness and productivity postconflict.

If this is correct, then forgiveness is not merely linked to positive effects but is a genuine source of these benefits. The results from the study suggest that if we focus primarily on the forgiver and their training, then the negative effects of workplace conflict will subside. Yet, as we will soon see, achieving these benefits requires much more than doling out forgiveness in the office.

IT TAKES A VILLAGE

Consider an unfortunately common case: imagine a workplace bully whose behavior is stressing you out and having a negative impact on your productivity. According to the studies, forgiveness is associated with decreases in stress levels and an increase in productivity. (Remember that this points to a correlation but not a causation.) Perhaps this might apply to your case too, and you should forgive the bully for mistreating you.

But even if forgiveness gives you the positive results in the beginning, they can't last. What if you continue to be mistreated? Or your boss does nothing about it? Or other employees refuse to take the behavior seriously? We do not need to engage in a yearlong study to tell us that this will almost certainly have a negative effect on your well-being and productivity. For this reason, the general link between forgiveness and positive office outcomes should not lead us to blindly promote forgiveness as a panacea to office conflict. We also must figure out the kind of work climate needed to allow for the possibility for forgiveness.[13]

Climate involves the shared values, work conditions, procedures, strategies, and types of engagement encouraged in the workplace. Although climate and culture are not synonymous, climate influences culture. When a climate is toxic—for instance, when verbal and emotional abuse become normalized and there is no system in place to express grievances—a culture of bullying develops over time. That is to say, an expectation of bullying emerges from the daily operations and values (climate) of an organization. What kind of work climate opens up the possibility for forgiveness?

Professor of management Ryan Fehr and colleagues suggest that a climate in which forgiveness emerges requires three cultural values: restorative justice, compassion, and temperance. When organizations implement work conditions, procedures, and strategies that are informed by these values, organizations can reduce conflict or at least make it possible for forgiving responses to emerge. Let's take a closer look at these values and examine how they can facilitate forgiveness.

Restorative justice entails the belief that resolving conflict requires the engagement of all stakeholders: victims, offenders, and other relevant parties. Rather than place the entire burden of conflict resolution on the victim's shoulders, restorative justice recognizes that other people have a role to play as well. Offenders apologize, supervisors offer restitution, and the organization as a whole works on rebuilding trust. Third parties may also be contracted to help resolve conflict.[14]

What might this look like in the case described above? Your bully could offer up an apology and compensate you. A manager could focus on what the organization could do to restore your well-being. You and your bully may be encouraged to engage in respectful dialogue mediated by a corporate representative or outside specialist, in order to figure out how best to proceed as co-workers. With restorative justice as a shared value, an organization involves everyone in the task of rebuilding and restoration. Distributing these burdens is both fair—the victim is not left to carrying this heavy burden all by himself—and makes it more likely that the victim will decide to forgive.

The value of compassion entails the shared belief in the importance of easing one another's pain. When expressing compassion, we recognize our shared humanity with others. We also refuse to see the wrongdoer only through their past actions. Instead we see them as possessing a holistic personhood. They are more than just their wrongdoing. When compassion is a shared organizational value, employees are less likely to seek revenge, take pleasure in someone's misfortune, or project their negative emotions and behavior onto bystanders.

Perhaps, if your workplace bully shared the value of compassion, he would refrain from being rude to spare you suffering. Your boss would have a serious conversation with the bully, explaining to him the suffering he is causing and reminding him of the importance of compassion to the organization. When compassion is shared in this way, conflict is less likely to arise. When it does arise, a victim is more likely to want to forgive.

A climate in which forgiveness emerges also requires the shared value of temperance. This value is concerned with restraining ourselves from disruptive and hurtful behavior even when we are tempted or provoked to act otherwise. It's about moderation, self-control, and self-mastery.

Ancient philosophers like Plato and Seneca thought that temperance dealt with the inner tension we feel between the rational and reasonable part of ourselves and the irrational, impulsive part. When we are temperate, we choose the rational and moral over the irrational and immoral. The ancients advise us that we can exercise temperance by figuring out which pleasures relate to our and others' well-being, and through practical wisdom choosing these pleasures over those that block or reduce well-being.[15] Some even suggest that temperance is the most basic value—the value on which all others depend.[16] It's hard to practice compassion when you would rather see other people suffer. And it's hard to share restorative justice as a value when you would rather engage in selfish or vengeful pleasures instead. According to this line of thought, to share the values of restorative justice and compassion requires us to have a certain amount of self-control. And temperance allows us to curb workplace conflict and respond to it in productive and selfless ways. To share temperance as a workplace value is to strive to choose nondisruptive behavior over the pleasure and immediate gratification that negative behavior and emotions may yield.

In a workplace where temperance is a shared value, your workplace bully will try to resist the temptation to mess with you in the first place. You, sharing in this value, will refrain from conspiring to make him pay. On an organizational level, leaders will model temperance by refraining from retaliation and avoiding negative responses to those under their leadership. The company might also create mindfulness training programs and classes to help employees deal with stressful events and tempting behavior. When temperance is a shared workplace value, it is likely to give people fewer things to forgive. It can also provide them with the motivation and incentive to choose moderate responses to wrongdoing over excessive, disruptive ones.

I would like to add one more cultural value that is not found on Fehr's list: patience. Patience involves endurance.[17] It's the ability to wait calmly despite delays and disruptions. We can be patient with victims when we wait calmly for them to forgive. We can also be patient with our own forgiveness. Patience also involves perseverance. It's the ability to remain attentive to a task over a long period of time. In this way, it's being patient with forgiveness itself. Engaging in moral practices of forgiveness (like moderating anger) with the aim of repair may require taking one's time. This may involve engaging in physical and reflective activities like therapy or daily mediation in which there are no quick fixes. Or it may require constant efforts to view the wrongdoer in a positive light. In sum, patience as a shared value comes with an appreciation for the fact that efforts at forgiving require undertaking certain steps carefully, and sometimes over long periods of time.

THE DARK SIDE

When organizations rush employees to forgive so that everyone can get back to being productive, this points to the dark side of forgiveness at work. As with the hurry-and-bury ritual I discussed in chapter 5, and the tendency we all have to experience the fallout fatigue I discussed in chapter 6, organizations may be tempted to ask or expect employees to forgive quickly so that the company can move forward.

Yet rushing employees to forgive puts unfair pressure on them. Moreover, it can encourage inauthentic acts of forgiveness. Fearing their boss's harsh judgment or collegial shunning, an employee claims to have forgiven even though the offense is still festering and the conflict has not been resolved. The benefits of forgiveness accrue only when forgiveness is freely given—yet a person who believes that their financial well-being depends on expressing forgiveness will feel immense pressure to forgive. Thus, organizational pressure is bound to fail and be counterproductive to the company's aims.

While organizations should expect that employees will generally get along with others, it is inappropriate for a company to pressure employees to forgive. "My boss pressured me to forgive" or "I was fired because I did not forgive" is a lawsuit waiting to happen. Organizations should promote values and create climates that encourage forgiveness, but they are stepping out of bounds when they rush and pressure employees to do it the forgiveness way.

Rushing employees to forgive also compromises their autonomy. Employees should have the freedom to choose when and how they deal with their own mistreatment. As I discussed in chapter 2, given our unique dispositions we will all respond differently to wrongdoing, and some will need longer than others to be ready to forgive (if they ever are). As long as employees are not being disorderly, violent, or vengeful, employers should be patient and give them the time they need.

A lack of patience can also reinforce abusive behavior. In the aftermath of wrongdoing, we unfortunately sometimes extend our patience to the wrongdoers rather than to the victim—

particularly if the wrongdoer has institutional power, like a CEO, or social power owing to their race or gender. When powerful employees engage in wrongdoing, oftentimes organizational leaders will be patient with their reformation. They will give them time to transform even while they continue to engage in disrespectful or unlawful behavior. At the same time, they will encourage victims to forgive by implicitly or explicitly pressuring them to quickly get over it. If companies sincerely want to create a climate ripe for forgiveness, they should resist these unfair, impatient, and coercive practices.

FORGIVENESS IS NOT THE ONLY ANSWER

I've noted that a certain kind of work climate can open the *possibility* for forgiveness. "Possibility" is key here. If organizational members share these values, then it becomes more possible for victims to forgive *if* they want to. However, these shared values can also open the possibility for other kinds of appropriate responses too. Hence, even if organizations succeed at creating what social psychologists and organizational specialists refer to as a forgiveness climate, achieving forgiveness should not be the only standard of postconflict success. To see this, let's return to our favorite workplace drama.

In the *Office* episode "Stress Relief" (2009), Dwight is concerned that his colleagues do not take fire safety protocols seriously even after he has preached the importance of this via PowerPoint. Believing that experience is the best teacher, he decides to start a fire. "This time," he muses, "smoking is going to save lives." Predictably, things go terribly wrong. As employees attempt to evacuate the office, every door handle is scalding hot (thanks to Dwight's use of a flame gun minutes prior). Screaming and panicking ensues upon the revelation that they are all trapped, surrounded by fire with no chance to escape. At this moment, Dwight acknowledges that it was only a drill. But it's too late. Stanley collapses with a heart attack. Michael tries to save him by declaring: "Stanley, you will not die! Barack is president. You are Black, Stanley."

The company's CFO reprimands Dwight and gives him two strikes. In addition to being required to apologize, Dwight is required to obtain signatures of his colleagues' forgiveness. Unsurprisingly, Dwight does not share in the values necessary for a climate of forgiveness. Instead of offering a sincere apology, he reads his statement of regret, which simply says: "I state my regret." Rather than show compassion for Stanley, Dwight blames him for what happened, claiming that "Stanley's heart attacked him." Unable to see how his actions made others suffer, he suggests that maybe next time there should be a bomb drill. Nor does Dwight show patience. After reading his statement of regret, he demands that everyone sign his forgiveness sheet. When they refuse, he finds clever ways throughout the episode to trick each of them into signing the form. The branch office lacks the climate that would open up the possibility for colleagues to forgive Dwight. There is no shared value of restorative justice. No mediator is called upon to help deal with their issue. While Corporate does have a meeting with Dwight, it's not a restorative justice meeting. None of his colleagues, except Michael, were invited to offer input on how to move forward.

Beyond lacking a climate conducive to forgiveness, Dunder Mifflin suffers from another problem: it believes that forgiveness is the only answer. Corporate's only standard for a peaceful resolution is documented proof of forgiveness. Perhaps the corporate managers read the aforementioned studies showing that forgiveness can contribute to employee retention and increased productivity. In any case, for the corporate managers at Dunder

Mifflin, workplace conflict— even the kinds that put employees' safety at risk and can cause heart attacks—can be resolved if employees express forgiveness. This is not a mistake that only fictitious corporations make. Many human resources departments, upper management, conflict scholars, and management experts also mistakenly believe that forgiveness is *the solution* to all problems in the workplace.

According to the management study conducted by Toussaint and colleagues, forgiveness is "the releasing of negative emotions and the extending of positive emotions, attitudes, and behavior toward the wrongdoer."[18] This may sound similar to the broad view of forgiveness, but it is quite different. Recall, the broad view has specific moral goals in mind such as reconciliation and release. The study's definition, by contrast, doesn't have any particular goal in mind—moral or otherwise.

Rather, forgiveness merely becomes an umbrella term under which a collection of benevolent actions and positive emotions are included. This seems to be a conceptual mistake: just because I smiled at you or act respectfully toward you does not mean that I have forgiven you. This is not to say that these actions aren't valuable. Indeed, they may be as valuable as forgiveness. But there is no need to conflate them with forgiveness. Even if you never forgive your co-worker, you might still extend to them empathy, kindness, or respect. These positive attitudes and behaviors do in fact contribute to a healthy workplace and, like forgiveness, should be acknowledged and promoted.

In developing their account of a forgiveness climate, the professors Ryan Fehr and Michele Gelfand similarly endorse a seemingly overly expansive concept of forgiveness. Forgiveness, on their account, is defined as "empathic, benevolent responses to conflict."[19] By casting such a wide net—including generally nonhostile responses to wrongdoing as forgiveness—they risk losing sight of the distinctive moral aims of forgiveness. Forgiveness might be *one* empathic, benevolent response. But it is one among many others. We should shine a light on them too. Forgiveness needn't be the lone strategy that organizations adopt to achieve the reparative results they want.

This is not to say that I am against forgiveness climates. Shared values are essential to responding to interoffice conflict. I'm only suggesting that you can share the values of a climate that facilitates coping with stress and pro-social outcomes without putting forgiveness on a pedestal as the singular aim of workplace conflict resolution. My worry is not simply that the concept doesn't capture all pro-social behaviors. More importantly, forgiveness may be too much to ask from employees. And because one needn't forgive in order to resolve workplace drama and get reparative results, we should encourage other options too.

In the same episode where Dwight demands forgiveness signatures, staff gather in the conference room for a guided meditation. They also participate in a comedy roast of Michael—at his request. These events are created to help them reduce stress and get back to being productive after the fire drill incident. As you can guess, more conflict arises. But the general idea here—that there are other ways to deal with stress and productivity in the workplace than for employees to forgive—is on the right track.

Often, employees may be more willing to participate in these other practices than to forgive an offender. Employees at Dunder Mifflin might never express their forgiveness by recording it on Dwight's signature sheet. But they can make use of meditative and laughter-inducing activities. We do better by employees by showing that a variety of coping strategies and benevolent responses are available, acceptable, and encouraged. If we put too much focus on forgiveness, we shift the burden of workplace well-being entirely to the victim. Instead we should allow the person who has been wronged the opportunity to engage in other pro-social responses. Recall from chapter 2 that a lack of forgiveness does not necessarily mean that a person is opposed to peace and resolution. Nor does it mean that they have chosen to engage in malevolence.

It's not that the resolution bar is too high. It's that forgiveness is not the only path to resolution.

If the productivity and well-being of employees is an organization's primary concern when dealing with conflict, organizations can be more effective by offering employees diverse coping strategies and expecting a range of benevolent responses—even if they don't take the form of forgiveness. We can lower our moral and emotional expectations of workers without lowering organizational goals.

I do think the values of forgiveness climates are worth retaining. But to eliminate any misconception about what we are encouraging and aiming for, let's forsake "forgiveness climate" language and replace it with something better.

I suggest that we replace the idea of "forgiveness climate" with "a climate of respectful cooperation." Rather than focus our workplace attention primarily on how to respond morally to wrongdoers, we ought to make sure that less wrongdoing occurs. Forgiveness looms less large when there are fewer things for employees to forgive.

In a climate of respectful cooperation, a person needn't rid themself of all negative emotions. Instead, they simply are required to treat others respectfully and to cooperate peacefully. This treatment involves a range of benevolent responses and behaviors. A climate of respectful cooperation creates an environment that facilitates and encourages such behaviors. It also shares in the values of restorative justice, compassion, temperance, and patience. But it does so with the aim that these values will make available a variety of strategies for coping with stress, along with other positive behaviors.

One of the main priorities in a climate of respectful cooperation is to curb and address the incivility that makes forgiveness relevant. When employees are disrespected, they are less creative and more likely to retaliate or quit.[20] As the professors of management and leadership Christine Porath and Christine Pearson observe, "just one habitually offensive employee critically positioned in your organization can cost you dearly in lost employees, lost costumers, and lost productivity."[21] So it pays to make this a priority.

One way to minimize incivility is for organizational leaders to model civility. This is not surprising. We model those in leadership and powerful positions—whether at home, in politics, or the workplace. If our leaders are uncivil and disrespectful, and we see that that's a way to advance or be heard, we are likely to follow suit. So, the first important step for organizational leaders is to make sure that they are setting an example by not being abusive, rude, or otherwise disrespectful.

In a climate of respectful cooperation, organizations also hire for civility. Leaders are careful about who they hire. If they detect incivility in an interview, they don't downplay or ignore it. They give it careful consideration.[22] When inquiring about an applicant's prior work experience, they want to know not just where and how long they've been employed, but also about the kind of person they were in those places. Were they toxic? Were they rude? Rather than hire for experience alone, a better approach is to also hire employees on the basis of past behavior and demonstrated civility.

Leaders also *reward* civility through job performance reviews and *penalize* incivility by taking complaints seriously, rather than evading confrontation and delaying resolution. A senior executive once reported, "Every mistake we've made in firing a questionable hire was in taking action too late, not too early."[23] Just as there are cues for bad habits—for instance, we might drink more in social settings or eat more when snacks are visible—uncivil people are cues for more incivility. A disrespectful person creates an environment of disrespect and ignites disrespect in others. Like excessive drinking and unhealthy snacking, sometimes it may be best to attack incivility at its source. Firing is one option to halt incivility. It can be difficult to fire, of course, in spaces such as academia, where tenure often protects persistently uncivil people from termination. But there are still options. Departments can limit the uncivil person's exposure to students or committees.

In policing incivility, we must be careful not to fall back on familiar double standards. In many professional domains, men are allowed to express anger at the office but women are not. White men are permitted to have temper tantrums but the same behavior would be unacceptable for employees of color. Or we might put up with the disruptive behavior of a boss but fire a low-ranking employee the first time they're disruptive. In a culture of respectful cooperation, incivility is dealt with in a fair way. When employees see that fair standards of civility exist and are rewarded, they are likely to respond to wrongdoing in civil and benevolent ways.

In addition to civility, a climate of respectful cooperation also promotes emotional intelligence, which also helps curb workplace conflict. In the leadership literature, emotional intelligence is often emphasized because it is thought to be a hallmark of effective leadership. But I think all employees can benefit from emotional intelligence, as it affects both one's inner life and one's outward behavior.

As I mentioned earlier, emotional intelligence is a set of skills that includes self-awareness, self-regulation, empathy, and social skills. Those who are self-aware have a deep understanding of themselves. Self-aware people are also aware of their emotions and how they influence other people. A self-aware person will recognize their emotions and attempt to either moderate them or use them constructively, instead of taking out on innocent co-workers their frustrations over being mistreated. Self-regulation is similar to the value of temperance, in that it involves managing oneself despite temptations to act otherwise. It's about choosing productive approaches rather than impulsive, disruptive ones. So even when a co-worker is uncivil, a self-regulated person—in a climate of respectful cooperation— is likely to respond with kindness instead of rudeness, even though they may feel tempted to be rude.

Empathy, as I discussed in chapter 6, involves imagining ourselves in the situations of others, and it also involves considering other people's feelings. An empathetic person acknowledges other people's fears or worries and listens to their concerns. This affects how they speak to others, solve problems, and manage teams. In a climate of respectful cooperation, employees will be encouraged, and expected, to speak to others with tact. When an employee brings a complaint against a co-worker and sees that their supervisor listens and shows concern for their well-being, the employee is likely to respectfully cooperate instead of sabotage others or act out in disrespectful ways.

Social skill is the ability to build bonds and maintain important connections with others. It's the ability to work and coordinate with others. Social skill does not require that everyone be an extrovert or a "people person." Rather, promoting social skill involves encouraging employees to connect and respectfully cooperate with others across different backgrounds and experiences, and despite past office offenses.

A climate of respectful cooperation will also benefit from emotional intelligence of another kind, which I refer to as *feminist emotional intelligence.*[24] This kind of emotional intelligence is the ability to be attuned to the ways in which gender, race, and their stereotypes can negatively affect how we read people's emotions and interact with them. Asking a woman co-worker if she is upset because she has her period, as Dwight did in the *Office* episode "Women Appreciation," would show a lack of feminist emotional intelligence. A person with feminist emotional intelligence will be vigilant to prevent stereotypes from affecting their behavior. When a co-worker brings a complaint against them, instead of assuming that they are acting emotional because they are a woman, or assuming they are overly aggressive because they are Black, an offender will listen and take them and their complaint seriously. This is likely to welcome a benevolent response from the aggrieved.

Lastly, in a climate of respectful cooperation, stakeholders are careful to make sure that they do not promote positive values that can obscure and invite wrongdoing. Recall that leaders can engage in the hurry-and-bury ritual, using forgiveness to cover up the wrongdoing of powerful CEOs. But forgiveness is not the only attitude that we misuse for unjust purposes in the workplace. We can also misuse resilience in a similar manner.

Resilience has become a hot topic in the field of management and leadership studies. The psychology professor Angela Duckworth, in her bestselling book *Grit*, defines resilience as passion and perseverance. Many have used the work of Duckworth and other writers on resilience to help them understand, for example, why top performers quit and how to help at-risk children succeed in education. The business world is also intrigued by resilience. In fact, there are currently about eight hundred articles on grit, and twelve hundred on resilience, on the website for *Inc Magazine*, one of the top business publications in America. A few years ago, while giving a talk on resentment and motivation to a business audience in Lisbon, Portugal, I was asked by an American entrepreneur if I would visit his company to talk about resilience. On balance, I think companies' interest in passion and perseverance, and their desire to impart these qualities to their employees, is a good thing. Businesses should want to teach their employees how to persevere through setbacks and disappointments, given that these are ubiquitous experiences in the workplace. But as with forgiveness, relying on resilience to solve workplace conflicts can itself be a source of significant problems.

Even though resilience is a good attitude to have when facing market obstacles, promoting resilience as a way to address workplace conflict obscures wrongdoing and encourages more bad behavior. Moreover, encouraging employees to persevere through unaddressed harassment, bullying, and disrespect is stress-inducing. Employees' resilience doesn't solve conflict. It may allow them to jump over it, but conflict will always remain unless it is dealt with effectively. This stress can build up over time and eventually explode into vengeance and division—far from the benevolent actions and respectful cooperation needed for any successful workplace. Although it may sound more empowering to motivate employees to persevere via forgiveness, organizations will do best to promote values that address wrongdoing rather than values that cover it up.

———

Forgiveness has become a buzzword in the business world. But like all buzzwords, it has lost much of its original meaning— while, unfortunately, other, more helpful alternatives have been forsaken. The workplace will benefit from recognizing that while forgiveness is one way to address incivility and wrongdoing, there are other effective and collaborative ways to do so too. It's important that we do not oversell forgiveness at the risk of encouraging misconduct, condoning the actions of bad actors, and limiting the range of options available to us for responding to conflict. Nor is responding to conflict and wrongdoing a task to be taken on only by victims. All members of an organization can and should work to promote a climate of respectful cooperation. As we will see in chapter 8, we can also benefit from this advice when we go online.

8

CANCELING VERSUS FORGIVING

IN 2016, Joanne the Scammer—a character portrayed by POC actor and comedian Branden Miller—became a viral video sensation. Donning a fur coat, blonde wig, and faux posh accent, the self-titled web series displayed her hilarious and obscene scams, as well as her self-centered, pretentious, and materialistic nature. In one episode, entitled "Caucasian Living with Joanne the Scammer," she engages in an MTV Cribs style tour of "her" mansion. It's clearly a scam. Pictures in the house are of a young white family, she has no idea where things are, and she steals jewelry as the tour proceeds—all the while confidently declaring to the camera man, "This is mine." At one point she offers to make him an espresso. However, she doesn't know how to work the machine, because . . . it's not hers! In frustration she declares, "That's over. It's canceled. We don't need coffee!"

Reflecting on the scene, episode writer Jason Richards noted how the term "canceled" fit perfectly in Joanne's world—a milieu of "reservations being canceled and credit cards being canceled. . . . It speaks to a lifestyle of commodity, consumerism and capitalism, of transactions being canceled," he said. "It's a very transactional word."[1] Following the episode, the use of "canceled" quickly increased in popularity online, particularly with Black users on Twitter (known as Black Twitter). Soon enough, the internet was awash in the cancellation of various items, companies, and people, though mainly celebrities. Some fans canceled the comedian Kevin Hart because of his homophobic tweets, and Dave Chappelle for his transphobic jokes. Some readers canceled the author J. K. Rowling for her transphobic tweets. Some listeners canceled the rapper Kanye West for his remark that "slavery was a choice."

The reality and risk of being canceled has not been received well by public figures—celebrities, politicians, journalists, authors, and so on. Even members of the public have expressed concerns about the unforgiving nature of what has become known as "cancel culture." Others have worried about the vengeful consequences this new "culture" welcomes—that it is "a direct assault on the construct of forgiveness."[2] In a recent interview the musician Demi Lovato urged listeners to opt for a "forgiveness culture" instead of a "cancel culture."

These are understandable concerns. A world in which we aren't allowed to make mistakes without a chance at redemption would be an awful place to live. And we can imagine the consequences that would arise if everyone around us were to valorize vengeful behavior and condemn people to punishments that do not fit their crimes. It is likely to create a social climate like the one to which the South African TRC was organized to respond. However, these concerns about canceling fail to grasp its true nature and the circumstances that bring it about. In this chapter, I will offer a defense of canceling, and argue that it is compatible with the aims of forgiveness. This will also be a limited defense: canceling is appropriate in the impersonal, commercial sphere, and has no place in our intimate relations.

WHEN TRANSACTIONS AND MORALITY MEET

Unfortunately, in modern parlance, the term "canceling" has become a catchall pejorative—used to describe all instances of criticism, particularly the piling-on, zero tolerance, career-destroying kind of online behavior. If we want to determine whether "canceling" is, in fact, incompatible with forgiveness, we need to develop a clearer sense of the term.

If canceling is a transactional word as Jason Richards notes, then it makes sense to cancel people with whom we have transactional relationships. Take the case of celebrities. As fans of comedians, writers, athletes, or musicians, we give our attention and money in exchange for entertainment. We choose to watch the Netflix standup comedy special in exchange for laughter. We choose to read the latest novel in exchange for literary drama. We pay hundreds of dollars to watch athletes fly high, dunk, and generally display abilities we only wish we had. We press play on the music streaming service app in order to listen to the musician's latest sonic creation with the hopes that it will make us dance or cry. Our relationship with celebrities, in contrast to our familial or platonic relationships, is purely transactional. For many fans, myself included, this is often hard to accept—particularly when considering my relationship with LeBron James.

Often our choices in this domain are commercial and artistic rather than moral. Our tastes determine, at least in most circumstances, which celebrities we give our money and attention to. The fact that you don't listen to John Coltrane might mark you as someone with poor taste, but it would be odd to suggest that it's immoral. Similarly, the choice to disengage with a particular celebrity—say, because they switch teams—is not necessarily the kind of choice that is open to moral criticism. We are free to both engage and disengage without being blameworthy.

But we also sometimes make these decisions for what are more clearly moral reasons. In the 1960s some boxing fans ended their transactional relationship with Muhammad Ali because of his opposition to the Vietnam war. More than a decade ago, I ended my transactional relationship with guitarist John Mayer because of offensive comments he made in a *Playboy Magazine* interview. I felt that I could no longer enjoy the voice of someone who expressed misogynistic comments about Black women like myself. In these cases, our moral views affect our aesthetic decisions. If a celebrity engages in what we take to be offensive or abhorrent behavior, then that may lead us to opt out of giving them attention, support, and money. We have a new term for this phenomenon—"canceling"—but the phenomenon itself is much older.

The media scholar Meredith Clark describes canceling as "an expression of agency, a choice to withdraw one's attention from someone or something whose values, inaction, or speech are so offensive, one no longer wishes to grace them with their presence, time, and money."[3] One reason we might withdraw our attention is because we want to avoid being complicit in supporting the person's abhorrent views. But as Clark notes, canceling can also be understood as an online accountability practice. It allows us to hold public figures morally accountable. In this way it is similar to the practice of calling out: calling attention to a person's morally problematic behavior. The point of the call-out, which often precedes the decision "to cancel," is to bring attention to the unjust actions of celebrities and to hold public figures to account—with the hopes that they will take responsibility and repent.

But who do fans think they are, one might ask? The behavior I have described so far sounds like unofficial moral policing that reeks of nosiness, self-righteousness, and grandstanding. Why should celebrities like Kanye West or J. K. Rowling be *our* targets? And why should we be their judge? Celebrities have an immense platform. By their very nature they are walking megaphones. A joke tweeted by a celebrity suggesting that they would kill their kid if they came out as gay is likely to have an impact that a comment by someone who is not a celebrity would lack. Not only would celebrities' words reach a larger audience, but the celebrities' status is likely to make others take their views more seriously—a young gay child, for instance, might be more likely to feel ashamed and vulnerable. As the superhero adage goes, "With great power, comes great responsibility." Moreover, celebrities' wealth and popularity often shield them from the normal mechanisms of interpersonal accountability, making it likely that they will repeat the behavior and it will be condoned—as happened with movie producer Harvey Weinstein, singer R-Kelly, and actor and comedian Bill Cosby, all of whose sexual misconduct had long been common knowledge in their industries. The call-out is a way to call attention to harmful behavior and to hold the celebrities morally accountable for their actions. If the celebrity refuses to change, canceling is likely to follow.

One criticism of canceling is that, as Angela Sailor has argued, "[canceling] seeks not to fix, but to destroy." She writes that canceling is "the poison that fatally blocks a prescriptive cure for human weakness."[4] I disagree. It's easy to come to Sailor's conclusion when we fail to see canceling as a practice of accountability or only in its extreme, zero-tolerance form. Coupled with the call-out, its purpose—rather than to destroy or forsake wrongdoers—is to criticize unjust or cruel behavior, with the aim of responding to and curing human weakness.

There are plenty of celebrities who, in the wake of public scandal, have admitted their mistakes, apologized, and vowed to do better. For example, when the American rapper Lizzo first released her song "Grrls" in 2022, disability advocates criticized her for using ableist language. Lizzo immediately offered an apology on twitter, changed the lyric, and rereleased the song. This kind of response, at least for some fans, provided sufficient reason not to withdraw their support. Afterward, many journalists analyzed why her apology was effective, and one described it as "a masterclass in taking ownership."[5] *Time* magazine suggested that workplace leaders can learn a lot from her apology.[6] Had she refused to admit wrongdoing or vowed never to change, it is likely she would have been canceled. This is what accountability is all about.

Of course, some fans are less forgiving. They believe that, even if the celebrity is contrite and accepts responsibility, they should not be afforded a second chance—the only acceptable solution is for the person to forfeit their career as a public figure. This is understandable when it is a response to criminal behavior like rape, domestic violence, or sex trafficking. But it seems extreme as a default response to celebrities' offensive lyrics, tweets, or jokes. We shouldn't forsake the practice because people can take it to an unpalatable extreme. We don't think that all forms of criticism, punishment, and calls for justice should be abolished simply because some people have taken them too far. Instead, we offer up norms that govern how people should conduct themselves. We say it's okay to criticize but not to dehumanize; it is okay to call for justice but not for violence. Likewise with canceling. In many instances, celebrities who are eventually canceled are those who fail to apologize, refuse to see the wrong in their actions, or continue to repeat their destructive behavior. When the celebrity does not properly respond to the call-out, canceling is often the final resort. In this way, far from being something that "fatally blocks a prescriptive cure for human weakness," canceling aims to hold humans accountable.

Some have compared canceling to boycotting. And there is no doubt it is akin to it. Rather than focus on businesses like traditional boycotting, canceling focuses on public figures, who are businesses unto themselves.[7] When Black citizens decided not to ride public buses in Montgomery, Alabama, in 1956 or support businesses in Birmingham in 1963 that enforced segregation laws, they were opting out of giving money and support to those who were complicit in their oppression. However, they did not boycott in order to destroy the city's economic system or to put local businesses out of business. The purpose of the boycott was to improve societal conditions by pressuring businesses to change their racist practices. Canceling is similar. Rather than being a practice that is about "destroying" the livelihood or reputation of celebrities, those who cancel often aim to protect the vulnerable, and to put fire under the feet of powerful people so that they can change their ways and so that oppressive systems, in general, can be dismantled. Citizens in Montgomery could have remained silent about their mistreatment, protested only in private, or discreetly stopped using public transportation. Instead they articulated their discontent and decision in order to bring attention to the injustice *and* to challenge segregationists to transform. Likewise, people can cancel celebrities and refrain from posting their decision online. Many in fact do. But those who announce their cancelation do it in order to *publicly* take a stand against injustice and to challenge public figures to change their ways. In this way, they aim for repair.

In contrast to the boycotts of the civil rights movement, which required immense coordination and resources, people today can engage in canceling with a touch to a screen. Social media has provided access to the public sphere—a chance to have one's voice heard—to many people who not long ago would have been excluded from the conversation. Public discourse, until recently, has predominantly been a discourse of the elite class to the exclusion of alternative voices.[8] But with the rise of social media, millions of "counterpublics" can now engage in debate, demand accountability, make appeals to justice, and publicly sever their relationships with public figures. Social media is a way for the marginalized—who are often the targets of ableist or sexist behavior—to push back against the powerful. This is particularly important when other institutions fail to do their part. When traditional standards of accountability fail, counterpublics rise to the occasion (via digital calls for accountability). These online communities allow individuals to express their agency through a refusal to give attention and support to people who express disrespect for them or for others.

As much as canceling is about agency, justice, accountability, and refusal, it is also about dissociation and solidarity. I liken it to what the philosopher Thomas Hill refers to as "dissociation from evil." Hill argues that one of the reasons we protest, even when it's likely that we may not be successful, is to dissociate ourselves from evil. And we dissociate not to wash our hands clean from sin, or to merely show that we do not share the same values as the racist, homophobic, or misogynistic celebrity. Often, it has less to do with us or the wrongdoer, and more to do with sufferers—victims of the behavior. Hill claims that "the

point of disassociation . . . is not so much to gain benefits for
oneself or to punish the corrupt but to enable one to honor the
persons, groups, and causes that, from a moral point of view,
most deserve it. One would disassociate from evil so that one
could more meaningfully associate with good."[9] Our attention
has currency. It matters, to what and to whom we give our attention. Canceling can allow us to take our currency away from
people who engage in the abuse and marginalization of others
and give it to more deserving folks. In doing so, we show our
solidarity with them in the struggle.

THE TWO CULTURES

As I argued in chapter 2, a person can have good reasons to
withhold their forgiveness. The decision to withhold forgiveness, far from being a moral defect, is often praiseworthy and
prudent. Given this, even if canceling involved a refusal to forgive, it would not necessarily be the horrible thing that some
make it out to be. But does canceling itself always involve a refusal to forgive? I doubt it. I can forgive an artist for their misogynistic or anti-Semitic comments and yet refuse to buy their
albums in the future. While I have moderated my anger toward
them with the aim of my own relief (an instance of forgiveness),
I can still choose to stop being a fan. This is akin to forgiving my
co-workers' harsh behavior and yet still choosing to resign from
the company. Those who participated in the boycotts during
the civil rights movement were also inspired by their leader,
Martin Luther King Jr., to forgive. For King, boycotting and an
ethic of forgiveness were compatible—indeed, he thought both
were necessary to achieve justice. The same is true with cultural
boycotts. Remember that, according to the broad view, forgiveness has several aims. Reconciliation is one aim among others.

Not every instance of forgiveness requires that we ride off into the sunset together.

Even if there's nothing inherently wrong with canceling, a person could still think that there are better alternatives, such as mercy and forgiveness. Perhaps this is why Demi Lovato urges us to choose a mercy / forgiveness culture over a cancel culture. But is this something we really want? To decide, we need to think carefully about the relationship between mercy, forgiveness, and canceling.

Mercy involves treating someone less harshly than you have a right to. By asking for mercy, a wrongdoer asks the victim to treat the wrongdoer less severely than is warranted by their wrongdoing. What is the relationship between mercy and forgiveness? They aren't necessarily linked. I can forgive you (that is, let go of anger; no longer have contempt; shake hands; view you in a new light) and extend mercy. But I can also forgive you without extending mercy. I can, for instance, forgive you, even if I prefer that the law still gives you a sentence that fits your crime, or if I decide to divorce you. This does not make the forgiveness less authentic.

Is it also true that one can extend mercy but withhold forgiveness? Yes. I can extend mercy because I am tired, I pity the offender, or I no longer want to deal with them. My merciful response doesn't require that I engage in any moral practice with a reparative aim.

How about canceling and mercy? While Lovato implies that these are mutually exclusive options, I think that mercy and canceling can and often do coexist. Consider this: If mercy involves treating someone less harshly than we have a right to, then we should ask ourselves: What level of harsh treatment does a fan have a right to? Without this answer, we cannot confidently know what counts as a merciful or merciless action.

Perhaps—on a scale of 1 to 10 of apt harshness—demanding refunds ranks as a 7, while creating a blog where you provide a hundred reasons the public should not support the artist ranks as a 9. In comparison, no longer supporting the artist's career would seem to rank much lower. Now, these specific rankings are a bit fanciful—as is the idea that we could specify harshness with a cardinal scale—but the point is that mercy is still compatible with harsh behavior. It is merely behavior that is less harsh than fans have a right to. And if so, though canceling may be "harsh," this doesn't mean it is therefore merciless.

Judges, for instance, sometimes give offenders lesser sentences than they have a right to give them. The offender is required to serve probation, say, rather than go to jail. When judges do this, we describe it as an instance of mercy. It is a merciful act, not because punishment is absent, but because the judge has a right to give the offender a harsher punishment but waives that right. This is all to say that mercy is not the absence of punishment, protest, consequences, or canceling. It can manifest despite the presence of punitive actions.

Even if all of this sounds correct, you might still think that there is something beneficial in promoting a culture of mercy or forgiveness. No one wants a culture in which we easily discard people and withdraw support from others, right? Don't we want a more merciful culture instead?

I think this opposition we have created between cancel culture and mercy / forgiveness culture is, on one level, unwarranted, because—as I've just argued—canceling, mercy, and forgiveness are not in conflict. But I also think that we shouldn't promote any of these as a "culture." When we turn canceling (or any practice, for that matter) into a culture, we will always endorse it without question or criticism. The problem of "culture" is not just the rate at which we uncritically engage. The problem is also the power of the crowd within the cultures. We can be led astray if we allow the size of the crowd to influence us in irrational ways. The mere fact that a large mass of people has canceled a celebrity does not give us reasons to also cancel that celebrity or withhold forgiveness. We should individually consider reasons for ourselves. The noise of the crowd shouldn't be the determining factor. Whatever decision you come to, though, make sure you act in ways that do not obscure, excuse, ignore, or perpetuate wrongdoing.

In this way, I am against cancel culture. But for similar reasons (related to rate, crowd, and lack of critical standards), I am also against mercy and forgiveness culture. I also think that when we present canceling, mercy, and forgiveness as competing options, we tend to make several mistakes.

First, those who present the "cancel culture" versus "mercy / forgiveness culture" dilemma often paint an extremely negative picture of canceling. When people suggest that we choose one or the other, they envision "cancel culture" in terms of mob-like piling on, virtue signaling, and people losing their livelihoods because of the reactions of a few zealous online fans. This is, however, a pejorative view of canceling. Perhaps there is a psychological tendency—exacerbated by the conditions of the internet—to abuse this otherwise justifiable practice. As I have argued, canceling is not, in practice, a vengeful, life-destroying enterprise—it is an accountability practice. And like any other practice, it can be abused and misused.

Those who present the dilemma also tend to paint an overly optimistic picture of mercy / forgiveness culture. Do we really want a world in which we respond to every wrongdoing with mercy and forgiveness—as we would do if we endorsed a mercy / forgiveness culture? There are reasons to be dubious. The British moralist Joseph Butler cautioned that we would never pursue justice if we allowed attitudes like pity, compassion, and mercy to be our primary responses to wrongdoing. To highlight this, he asks us to imagine a murder case.

> Let us suppose a person guilty of murder, or any other action of cruelty, and that mankind had naturally no indignation against such wickedness and the authors of it; but that everybody was affected towards such a criminal in the same way as towards an innocent man: Compassion amongst other things, would render the execution of justice exceedingly painful and difficult, and would often quite prevent it.[10]

Similarly, the philosopher Charles Griswold, in his important work on forgiveness, offers the following warning about forgiveness culture:

> When forgiveness becomes the public rallying cry, played out on daytime television soap operas, encouraged by civic and religious leaders, and praised far and wide for its power to heal, its slide into confusion and vulgarity is almost inevitable. It becomes identified with "closure," it is sentimentalized and transformed into therapy, and the criteria for its practice are obscured. It melds into forgetfulness of wrong, and is granted all to easily, once the expected public theatrics are performed.[11]

Griswold does not argue against forgiveness itself, but instead highlights the problems that are likely to arise if forgiveness became a culture. Forgiveness may be a good thing for many. But a culture of forgiveness much less so.

In my view, the fostering of cultures—whether they be cancel culture, mercy culture, or forgiveness culture—is not a good idea. This doesn't mean that we should never cancel or never extend mercy or forgiveness. When we are engaged in the business of holding others accountable and taking a stand against evil, we must make sure that we ourselves are being moral. In order to do so, we should work hard to practice the virtues of canceling and not its vices. We can do this by extending humility, empathy, and tact. We can do it by being sincere and honest. And we cancel virtuously by being discerning and critical of the information that comes our way.

CANCELING IN PRIVATE

It's worth noting that online canceling has been reserved mostly for the public sphere and in response to the immoral actions of the rich and famous—people we are unlikely to have met. How does canceling manifest in our personal lives? To conclude this exploration of canceling, I'll explain why the language and attitude of canceling is inappropriate for intimate relationships, and suggest that we would do better to use the language of forgiveness (or unforgiveness).

I began this chapter by noting how Joanne The Scammer's cancelation of an expresso machine helped to popularize the concept of canceling. However, it did not create it. The first appearance of canceling in pop culture occurs in the 1991 action crime film *New Jack City*. In one scene the drug kingpin Nino Brown is being chastised by his girlfriend—who is fed up with his murderous behavior. "You're a murderer Nino, I've seen you kill too many people!" He responds by pouring Moet on her dress while uttering the words: "Cancel that bitch. I'll buy another one." This particular usage has recently experienced a pop culture resurgence. A New Orleans rapper has described his decision to break up with his girlfriend by rapping, "I had to cancel that Bitch like Nino"; a reality TV star informed his own love interest that the relationship was over by telling her, "You're canceled."

The origin and above usages of the term are misogynistic. Women who are canceled (and women who are bought following the cancelation of previous women) are viewed as objects— things that can be purchased, like expresso machines, and easily returned when they don't bend to men's wills. This objectification is morally worrisome and socially unacceptable because women are not objects. Women are human beings with subjectivity and agency. But you don't have to cancel a woman for such behavior to be problematic. Any time we treat those close to us as objects in this fashion, we are not respecting them.[12] We could also be dehumanizing them.

Recall that canceling is a transactional concept. It refers to transactional relationships—relationships between consumers and the providers of cultural products. Our intimates are neither. This is not to say that exchange does not play a role in our intimate relationships. I expect my best friends to be honest with me. And they expect the same from me. If they are dishonest, I am justified in withdrawing my trust. You expect your partner to provide emotional support. And they expect you to do the same. If they refuse to help or disappear during a moment of psychological hardship, you are justified in revaluating the relationship or questioning whether you should be available for them in similar ways. However, the existence of these exchanges doesn't make the relationship transactional. It makes it a *reciprocal relationship*.

Reciprocal relationships, as I see them, are relationships that involve mutual respect and mutual expectations between individuals. And the fulfillment of these expectations is what allows each person to become better, and the relationship to function better. Mutual expectations can include things like honesty, love, understanding, commitment, compromise, and appreciation. A healthy relationship will not exist if these qualities are absent or if only one person extends them. It requires both parties to hold up their end—that is to say, it requires reciprocity.

When we make our intimate relationships transactional instead of reciprocal, we run into all sorts of problems. Instead of extending mutual respect, we can engage in disrespect. Nino Brown is unable to receive his lover's criticisms with humility and understanding, in part, because he thinks of their relationship as transactional. To him, she is his showpiece. She should do what he says. If she malfunctions—that is, no longer does what he wants—he can get rid of her in the most humiliating way. Forgiving her is never an option. But we needn't emulate Nino Brown's actions to be disrespectful via canceling. We can just mimic our own online behavior.

Let's say that a friend of ours has been acting quite mean recently. Being fed up with their behavior, we call them out on it. However, they neither acknowledge their behavior nor repent. We then decide to tell them, "You're canceled!" and never speak to them again. What could possibly be wrong with that?

Well, the phrase itself can communicate, if only implicitly, that they are objects and that our relationship is transactional. But also, withdrawing from the relationship in this manner doesn't seem fitting in our personal lives. In contrast to celebrities, with whom we have the thinnest of commercial relationships, our relationships with friends carry certain obligations. Before we disassociate—given the friendship—we should attempt to find the cause behind their unkindness. We should want to know why their behavior has recently changed. Perhaps they are extremely depressed, overwhelmed, grieving, or stressed. Although this is not an excuse for the behavior, it would make us more empathetic. Helping them deal with their grief may assist them with curbing the mean behavior—this may be more productive than calling out their behavior. This understanding may also give us a reason not to withdraw from the relationship just yet.

But what if their behavior is beyond the pale—not merely mean but racist or misogynist? And what if it's not owing to any emotional challenges? Don't we have a right to call them out and then cancel them if they do not repent? As I have defined canceling, it's conceptually impossible to "cancel" our friends, because we do not have a transactional relationship with them. Acting as if we do is to treat them as objects—canceling would be an inappropriate response. The intimate nature of our relationship will require us to follow a different script than public discursive practices directed at celebrities whom we don't know personally. Perhaps, instead of instantly canceling them, we extend patience. And this could be because they once were patient with us during a rough period, and we saw how it helped us improve. We can give them a little bit more time without condoning their actions. If they do not change, then we will dissociate from the relationship. However, I do not think this would be a case of canceling. It would be an instance of unforgiveness.

The language of forgiveness / unforgiveness more accurately captures what's happening than does the idea of canceling. Suppose, despite our disapprobation and rebuke, our friend continues to think that it is okay to use the N-word to refer to African Americans. In response, we maintain our anger at her and refuse to repair the relationship. Or we refuse to attend any events where she is present so that she and others will not mistake us for endorsing her offensive and unrepentant behavior. We also do this so that she will not feel relief from a sense of wrongdoing and harm. Canceling doesn't fully capture what's happening. We are not simply withdrawing support because she did not take responsibility for her actions. Nor are we, like a fictitious drug kingpin, instantly replacing her as a penalty or reminder of her low status. We are, instead, refusing to engage in a certain set of moral practices with a certain moral aim. And this is owing to our friend's unapologetic wrongdoing. This is best described as a refusal to forgive, or a case of unforgiveness. This also avoids the implication that we view our friends as disposable objects.

———

When our favorite celebrities engage in immoral behavior, we all face a decision of what to do. We might forgive and continue in the transactional relationship or leave it. This latter option is possible, I have argued, because canceling public figures is compatible with forgiveness. Or we might withhold forgiveness yet end the relationship. This is possible because forgiveness does not entail reconciliation. While neither decision is wrong per se, they can go awry when we decide to cancel out of self-righteousness, a disregard for the facts, or feeling pleasure at someone's downfall.

The defense of canceling I have offered is limited to our transactional relationships. We should resist bringing canceling into our private lives. Perhaps the best thing we can do to escape treating our intimates as objects is to forsake "cancel" language and focus on forgiveness: "I forgive you but can no longer support you" or "I don't forgive you and I never want to see you," to name a couple of options. Regardless of our choice of language, we must not lose sight of the fact that we all have a role to play in the work of repair. This work can be all the more challenging when it comes to forgiving ourselves.

9

FORGIVING YOURSELF

NOT A DAY GOES BY that I do not think of my deceased mother. My thoughts in part are owing to grief. I miss our conversations, her hugs, and her unconditional love. I would do anything to bring her back. The other thoughts I have are rooted in regret. I wish I had been a better daughter. I wish I had been more attentive to her needs. I wish I had visited her more often. I wish . . . It has been much easier to forgive my stepfather than it has been to forgive myself.

It makes sense, conceptually, for us to forgive or withhold forgiveness from selfish and inconsiderate wrongdoers. But things get more complicated when that wrongdoer is oneself. What gives us the right to forgive ourselves? The purpose of presenting the broad view of forgiveness is not just to expand what we take forgiveness to be. It's also to broaden the scope of who has the right or standing to forgive. On the narrow view, only victims can forgive wrongdoers. But on the broader conception, this right extends to wrongdoers (forgiving themselves). Self-forgiveness is possible. This doesn't mean, however, that it's without difficulties or dangers. But it is possible.

GETTING BEYOND THE FANTASY

Forgiving others and forgiving yourself involve similar practices and aims. There are subtle differences, though. Some of the differences can be explained by the fact that the target of forgiveness is oneself. Forgiving yourself can involve, among other practices, relinquishing shame, overcoming negative self-evaluations, or refraining from self-harm.

We forgive ourselves so that we might achieve several self-directed reparative aims. We can forgive in order to get release from the offense, get relief from self-hatred, or to reconcile ourselves to ourselves so that we can go on living. These self-directed aims might even be required in order to repair our relationship with a victim—for it may be hard to reconcile a friendship when we have refused to forgive ourselves. In order for repair to be achieved among friends, it must also occur within the offending friend. Myriad things can be the objects of forgiveness. You can forgive yourself for having performed bad deeds and having had cruel thoughts. You could forgive yourself for harboring hatred and contempt and for what you could have done but neglected to do.[1] Whether we have the standing to forgive ourselves is another question. If we don't have this right, then self-forgiveness is just a fantasy. If we do, then it is not only possible but requires that we perform it with much care.

Dostoyevsky's philosophical novel *The Brothers Karamazov* directly tackles the issue of who has the right to forgive. (As we will see, it's helpful for answering our self-forgiveness question.) The topic of forgiveness occurs in the novel during a conversation about the problem of evil. Ivan, in talking with his monk brother, Alyosha, cites the suffering of children as a counterexample to the idea that there is harmony in the universe. He denies that parents, in responding to their children's suffering, can forgive the perpetrators. "But the sufferings of her tortured child she [the mother] has no right to forgive; she dare not forgive the torturer, even if the child were to forgive him!"[2] This standing question also extends to God. When discussing the suffering of a child torn to pieces by hounds at a master's command, Ivan asks, "What right does God have to forgive such a monster when it wasn't God who was torn to pieces?" For Ivan, because the mother and God did not suffer what the child suffered, they have no right to forgive the offender for the child's suffering.

We can see how this might also apply to self-forgiveness. Who are we to forgive ourselves for the sufferings we've inflicted on others? We ourselves did not suffer, so it appears—based on Ivan's logic—that we have no right to forgive. The philosopher Gordon Marino agrees. In describing self-forgiveness as a fantasy, Marino recognizes that changing yourself and recognizing wrongdoing is one thing. Forgiving yourself is another. He urges us "to preserve the distinction."[3]

There is no consensus on this issue among philosophers of forgiveness. For some thinkers, only victims can forgive. Because the wrongdoers are not the victims, they have no right. Only victims can forgive offenders for the suffering they've endured at offenders' hands. Thus, self-forgiveness is impossible at best and inappropriate at worse. These thinkers don't believe that your boss can forgive your co-worker for bullying you or that a daughter can forgive her stepfather for cheating on her mother. Forgiveness belongs only to the victim. Ignoring this "risks appropriating and even silencing the victim's voice. . . . third-party efforts involve, at best, a dangerous paternalism; at worse, they are morally and logically incoherent."[4] On the other hand, there are philosophers who believe that self-forgiveness is possible and thus appropriate (under certain conditions). I am part of this latter camp. To make sense of the possibility of self-forgiveness, it helps to begin by laying out the harms that self-forgiveness responds to. This will help determine if it is a paradox or a possibility.

Self-forgiveness responds to harms done to others and harms done to ourselves. Self-forgiveness seems more coherent when it comes to self-harm, because in this case the forgiver is also the victim. If, as Ivan and some philosophers claim, only victims can forgive, then self-forgiveness is possible. It's possible as a response to self-harm. There are many ways we can harm ourselves. We can engage in self-degradation, including behavioral practices—such as letting ourselves become addicted to drugs—where we "demean . . . or damage our capacities."[5] We can also sacrifice our own hopes and plans through irrational or poor short-term decision making. When we begin to forgive ourselves for these harms, we are responding as an agent to our own victimhood.[6] In response to our self-infliction of harm, we say "I forgive."

Understanding self-forgiveness gets trickier when it comes to harming others. There is a variety of ways in which we can hurt other people. I needn't provide a list for you here. A stroll through social media or cable news channels reveals the various sufferings we enact on each other every day. Whether it's neglect, verbal abuse, disrespect, violence, or injustice, we have all harmed others at some point in our lives. Is it possible to forgive ourselves for it? Thinkers like Marino don't think so. But this position has more to do with how we conceive of harm than it does with forgiveness itself.

Those who think that only victims can forgive have what the psychologist Sharon Lamb refers to as a "hyperindividualized notion of personal harm."[7] They believe that the only people who can be harmed by an offense are the victims who suffer as a direct result of the offense. These victims are direct or primary victims. Often, however, there are multiple kinds of victims of wrongdoing, various people who experience harm as a result. The mother in Ivan's story did not suffer in the way her child did, but she did suffer the loss of a child. That is a harm that is hers alone. It's for this reason that Ivan also says, "Let her forgive him for herself, if she will, let her forgive the torturer for the immeasurable suffering of her mother's heart." The murder of a child does not only affect the child. The murder has multiple victims, his mother being one of them. Therefore, it's possible for the mother to forgive the murderer. She is forgiving him not for the same reasons for which her son would. But her forgiveness is possible. This distinction helps makes self-forgiveness more coherent.

If there are multiple victims of personal harm, it's also possible that the wrongdoer *might* be one of the victims. This rings particularly true if you agree with the ethical viewpoints of James Baldwin and Martin Luther King Jr. Baldwin thought that hatred is always self-hatred, and that "whoever debases others is debasing himself."[8] King believed that "we are caught in an inescapable network of mutuality, tied in a single garment of destiny. Whatever affects one directly affects all indirectly."[9] If by hurting others, we also hurt ourselves (although not to the same degree)—as Baldwin and King communicated so eloquently—then it makes sense that a person could forgive themself for inflicting such harm. A daughter could forgive herself for depriving herself of precious time she could have spent with her mother. A misogynist could forgive himself for allowing his sense of inferiority and his need for control to destroy his valuable relationships. Note, as Ivan makes clear in his analysis of the mother and child, that we forgive ourselves for ourselves, for the torture of our own hearts. Only the victim has the right to forgive for their own suffering. Forgiving on their behalf and forgiving oneself for what you did to them are distinct. This leads us to another reason self-forgiveness is possible.

The philosopher Alice MacLachlan argues that third parties can forgive based on their relationship of care and solidarity with the victim.[10] This relationship is based on being committed to the victim's interests. Examples of third parties who stand in this relationship and therefore would have the right to forgive are family and friends.

According to this view, a mother can forgive her child's murderer. She can forgive the wrongdoer not only for the loss of her child but also for violating the interests of her son—interests to which the mother was committed. A daughter can forgive her stepfather for violating her mother's interests, to which the daughter was also committed. In this way, the daughter and grieving parent can forgive because they have taken the harm personally. They are forgiving the wrongdoer for the harm inflicted on someone they love. The harm affects them intimately.

Third parties also include members of minority communities who share social and political identification and allegiances with the victim. On this account, members of the Black community in Harlem can forgive a white supremacist murderer in South Carolina. This is because members of that community are invested in the Black victims' survival. Their forgiveness is born out of their relationship of solidarity with the victim. This doesn't mean that their forgiveness can substitute for the victim's. It simply means that they have the standing to forgive or withhold forgiveness, given this relationship.

How does third-party forgiveness relate to self-forgiveness? It is possible for wrongdoers who stand in a relationship of care with their victim to forgive themselves for violating their beloved's interests (to which they were committed). I can forgive myself for the mean things I said to a close friend because I stand in a relationship of care to her and I violated her happiness, safety, peace, and protection—to which I was committed.

There's one additional reason self-forgiveness is possible. Recall that forgiveness involves the letting go of, or foreswearing, negative emotions and attitudes—although it's not limited to these practices. We often resent ourselves for what we said to a loved one; for how we treated a friend; for what we failed to do concerning a co-worker. If this resentment is possible, then the relinquishment of resentment via forgiveness is also possible. Self-forgiveness, then, would involve the letting go of negative emotions directed at ourselves. If we contain multitudes (I can be a nice, compassionate person one day and a cruel, rude person the next), then it's possible for the person I've become today to stop resenting the cruel person I was yesterday.[11]

"Thinking about your past self in this way does not imply that there are literally two people involved," explains the philosopher Peter Goldie. "You now are the very same person that you were then, and it is precisely because of this that self-forgiveness is possible. . . . The possibility of self-forgiveness and redemption, then, arises just because you can see your earlier self from the perspective of a renewed, changed self, who is now able to rejoin the moral community."[12] If forgiveness can occur when we give up resentment toward others, it can also occur when we stop resenting our former selves.

In sum, self-forgiveness is possible because wrongdoers can also be victims, stand in a relationship of care with victims, and resent themselves.[13] Just because self-forgiveness is possible, however, doesn't mean it's easy, or harmless, or that we should extend it freely. As Goldie states: "We need to allow ourselves the possibility of self-forgiveness, achieved in the right way and at the right time, in order to be able to get on with our lives, and not to damage the lives of others who are close to us."[14]

THE DIFFICULTIES AND THE DANGERS

Forgiving yourself for harming others and for harming yourself both come with their own difficulties. When attempting to forgive ourselves the suffering we have caused others, we might feel so ashamed about what we've done that forgiveness is extremely difficult. Shame makes us want to hide, and it is difficult to address our past actions when we are hiding from ourselves. Shame can also make us lash out defensively. We can get caught up in defending ourselves instead of facing what we've done. As long as shame remains, repair can never begin. While it might seem that getting rid of negative emotions like shame might do the trick, it would be a mistake to try to get rid of all negative emotions. Guilt is often good for the wrongdoer. Embracing guilt is a bit healthier than shame.[15]

As one philosopher put it, with guilt we submit to our own or other people's anger, but with shame we submit to their contempt.[16] In other words, when we feel guilt, we accept that anger in response to our actions is warranted. Through the acceptance, we own up to what we've done and confirm that it was indeed a bad thing to do. When we feel shame, we give in to our own and others' disdain and hatred. This is likely to make repair via forgiveness difficult, because we will not think we are worthy of forgiveness. Perhaps this is why the actor Will Smith, in his first YouTube video uploaded after the 2022 Oscars controversy, said, "I'm trying to be remorseful without being ashamed of myself. I'm trying not to think of myself as a piece of shit."[17]

In addition, guilt focuses on what we've done, whereas shame focuses on who we are. It's much more difficult to forgive yourself when you feel shameful about who you are as opposed to guilty for what you've done. This focus on ourselves as bad people instead of bad doers can lead to unfair punishment. When you think your actions define all of who you are, it is difficult to find a piece of you that is worth redeeming. Guilt can also motivate us wrongdoers to account for what we've done.[18]

It can also lead us to outward action. Because guilt is unpleasant, we seek ways to relieve ourselves of it through apologies and compensation. Guilt can also promote good deeds. The social psychologist Mary B. Harris and colleagues conducted a study to test whether confession reduces guilt and therefore altruism. They set up March of Dimes donations sites at the entrance and exit of a Catholic Church during confession hour.[19] What they discovered was that people were more willing to donate money prior to confession. The researchers concluded that the participants gave more money on their way to confession because they were feeling guilt. They gave less money after confession because their guilt had been relieved. The researchers concluded that, indeed, confession (as a way of reducing guilt) reduces altruism. Guilt, therefore, increases altruistic behavior. Not only is guilt healthy for the wrongdoer; it can benefit others. This is not to say that guilt can't be excessive, making it unhealthy for all. It is only to suggest that we embrace a healthy form of guilt, given these benefits—and reject shame, which gets in the way of repair.

Self-alienation is another difficulty we might face when attempting to forgive ourselves. It is tempting to stay in the past, remain horrified at what we've done, and continue to ruminate on our behavior. This leads us to play the "What If" game. What if we had thought about this, or had done that? (Repeat). Our rumination might even be in good faith—we do it to show the victim that we have not forgotten the horrible things we've done. However, this game is bound to keep us in the past in negative ways, as opposed to focusing on the future. If we stay in the past, we will never forgive ourselves. Acting in the present and attempting to create a better future is a way to escape self-alienation. Forward-looking actions are our best options. They include fulfilling our obligations, such as making amends. And avoiding repeating our mistakes.[20]

Forgiving ourselves can also be difficult when we engage in irrational forms of self-blame. This can happen when we weigh the harm we've done as being more severe than it is. We can beat ourselves up for failing to do something minor and then conclude that we are the most irresponsible student ever, the worse mother of all time, or so horrible that no one should be our friend. We can also blame ourselves for things that we are not responsible for. While we may be responsible for disappointing a friend, this doesn't mean that we let all of our friends down. The fact that we were dishonest with a person ten years ago doesn't mean that we are responsible for their life having recently fallen apart. This is not to say that we must not think about the repercussions of our actions, no matter how small we judge our wrongdoing to have been. Instead, it is important to encourage what the philosopher Kathryn Norlock calls "rational forms of self-blame."[21] They invite accurate self-reproach that is healthier and more likely to lead to self-forgiveness.

This form of self-reproach is a balance. The philosopher Robin Dillon explains this middle ground as follows:

> Self-forgiveness does not require extinguishing all self-reproach, for it is not really about the presence or absence of negative feelings and judgements; it's about their power.

Forgiving oneself means not that one no longer experiences self-reproach but that one is no longer in bondage to it, no longer controlled or crippled by a negative conception of oneself and the debilitating pain of it, no longer alienated from oneself, so that one can now live well enough. This is possible even if one retains a measure of clear-sighted self-reproach, overcoming it without eliminating it.[22]

An accurate form of self-approach is not only a better representation of the past; it's also a better way to treat ourselves, manage our emotions, and move forward.

Even if we can escape the difficulties that come with forgiving ourselves, self-forgiveness isn't always appropriate. Self-forgiveness is inappropriate when it occurs without repentance. Repentance is necessary for self-forgiveness. Repentance involves a change of heart. Without it, we are merely acting out of arrogance when we forgive. The philosopher Anthony Bash goes even further: "Those who 'self-forgive,'" he writes, "if they have not repented engage in an act of enormous selfishness and egoism that, at the expense of moral integrity, seeks to ease a troubled conscience, denies responsibility, or indicates a person with a conscience that is pathologically self-absorbed and narcissistic."[23]

The philosopher Espen Gamlund also thinks self-forgiveness should only occur after repentance. But for it to be appropriate, the wrongdoer must do more. He must "ask the victim for forgiveness before considering whether to forgive himself. The reason for this is that the act or process of self-forgiveness cannot be a one-sided affair. . . . It is the victim who has been wronged and the victim should therefore be the first person to consider whether or not the wrongdoer should be forgiven."[24]

Addressing the offense is an essential first step to self-forgiveness. It involves taking responsibility, showing remorse, and engaging in repentance. I disagree with Gamlund, however, as it relates to asking for forgiveness. It is true that self-forgiveness cannot be one-sided, and that it should have some involvement from the victim. It's the nature and degree of this involvement that I am concerned about. Gamlund thinks we should ask the victim for forgiveness before forgiving ourselves. I, on the other hand, think it is best that the wrongdoer expresses a hope for forgiveness rather than ask for it (for the reasons I address in chapter 3). But Gamlund thinks the victim's involvement is not limited to simply granting forgiveness:

> He [the wrongdoer] will need forgiveness to move on with his life, to regain a sense of self-respect and self-worth. He will need confirmation from the victim that he is not a bad person; that the wrong he did does not stem from a permanent defect in his character. He will need the victim to tell him or communicate to him—through her forgiveness—that he is a human being with human dignity and worth. He will need affirmation from the victim that she will not hold against him what he did in the future, that he will not have to carry his burden of guilt with him forever. In short, the repentant wrongdoer will need to be forgiven by his victim.[25]

I am exhausted reading all the needs a victim is supposed to satisfy via forgiveness. This is too much work for the victim and too much to expect forgiveness to accomplish. As I've argued throughout this book, victims already take on so much. We must be careful not to overburden the victims in the aftermath. There are lots of things that we may want from a victim. Not all of these wants equate to needs. I think that, minimally, in certain contexts and after careful consideration, we should express remorse to victims, repentance, and a hope for forgiveness. But we must remember that this may not be welcomed in every circumstance. Some victims want nothing to do with us. To beg for their involvement despite this fact is disrespectful. If the victim does not satisfy our wants, but we have taken responsibility, repented, and have considered the victim, the gravity of the harm, and timing—we should begin the journey toward self-forgiveness. It would be awful to think that my stepfather's self-forgiveness depended on my forgiveness. That is to grant me too much power. It's a power I do not want. To be sure, philosophers agree that granting forgiveness is an exercise of moral power. I do not deny this. The power I am concerned with here is one that is exclusively mine and that overrides offenders' willingness to repair their lives. On the other hand, self-forgiveness gets dangerous when we think it can substitute for the victim's forgiveness. The acceptance and grace we give ourselves is not the same as what can be given by the victim, nor is it a replacement. To think that it can replace their forgiveness is to disregard victims' agency.[26] My stepfather's self-forgiveness is not a replacement for my mother's or my own forgiveness.

Irrational forms of self-blame involve not only being too hard on oneself, but also being too easy on oneself. Irrational self-blame is a danger we must avoid. When we forgive ourselves without any difficulty and quickly—because we don't really see our past actions as harmful, or we see victims as somewhat responsible for the wrong—it's clear that we're being too easy on ourselves. Seeing the victim as partly responsible for the wrong is an example of victim blaming. We inaccurately present our wrongdoing as less severe because we have assigned some form of undue blame to the victim. We might say, "They let me do it," or "It's their fault they were in the wrong place at the wrong time," or "They should've complied," to make our harm seem less severe. To escape this danger, we must face the hard truth of what we've done, while being careful not to be too hard or too easy on ourselves. I admit: this is a difficulty in and of itself.

Another danger we should stay clear of is abdication. We must be careful not to use self-forgiveness to relinquish our responsibilities. You can imagine a person who says, "I already forgave myself" in response to a request to pay reparations or accept a fair punishment. They are using self-forgiveness to shut down any further discussion about their past actions. Their self-forgiveness—rather than the offense—becomes the headline. This is like celebrities using their public apologies to appropriate the narrative, as I have discussed in chapter 3. We must resist using self-forgiveness to distract attention away from our having committed blameworthy actions. Instead, we should use it to make amends.

THE CURIOUS CASE OF REGRET

There is a misconception about forgiveness that is hidden in popular metaphors and clichés. Consider "Forgive and forget" and "Wipe the slate clean." Though these phrases convey two different ideas, they are similar in that when we express them, we are assuming that once forgiveness has taken place, newness awaits. The past no longer negatively impacts the future. You can forgive and have no memory of the wrongdoing. You can wipe your slate clean and leave no dirty residue behind. Of course, this is false. If anything is a fantasy, it is the idea that nothing painful is left over after forgiveness. Self-forgiveness can make way for relief, release, and reconciliation. It can also leave residue.

The philosopher Claudia Card refers to this residue as "moral remainders." Just as hard work doesn't always give us neat results, moral remainders can persist after we've made the hard commitment to forgive ourselves; revealing that reparative action can still leave breaks and cracks behind. Moral remainders are emotions and attitudes that stay with us after forgiveness has occurred. Regret and remorse are common examples. Out of the two, Card notes, "forgiveness relieves neither."[27] Regret and remorse "remain even after we've done all we can do to set things right."[28] Self-forgiveness doesn't mean the absence of regret.

Regret is "sorrow over a fault, offense, mistake or loss, ranging in intensity from mild to deep."[29] You can feel regret even when you are not responsible for what happened—as when you regret that you were not around when a terrible event occurred, believing that you could have prevented it if you had been there. This is part of the regret I have concerning my mother. I wish I had been there the day she fell ill at home alone. But when, in contrast, you are responsible for wrongdoing and the regret becomes intense, you experience remorse. Remorse is a deeper form of regret. According to Card, it's an "intense, often lasting, moral regret regarding one's own conduct."[30] When we experience remorse, we "profoundly wish we had not done a wrongful deed, not because of the stain on our own character but because of how it wronged others."[31] I feel this deeper form of regret for not having been the best daughter I could have been, for not having given my mother the attention she deserved. I wish I had acted differently, that I had been more responsible. I am aware that she felt my neglect. The painful knowledge of it is heartbreaking. These feelings can creep up at any moment. The philosopher Kathryn Norlock refers to the recollections that accompany both remorse and regret as "intrusive memories."[32] Mine are invasive indeed. Out of nowhere—while I'm reading a book, playing video games, listening to music—remorse and regret can gnaw at me. But I have forgiven myself. Why do I still have these feelings? What is the purpose of all this pain?

Moral regret (as distinguished from the regret we feel for not going to a concert) signals our values. It advertises what we stand for. More specifically, it reveals that we acknowledge our wrongdoings and shortcomings. It shows that we recognize, as Card puts it, "that all has not been made right, or that not all is as it should be (or would be, ideally) between us."[33]

I understand now why I've always been suspicious of people who live by the motto "No Regrets." If the purpose of regret is to signal that we acknowledge wrongdoing, then a person who never experiences regret may have never taken responsibility for their actions. Perhaps it's because they believe they've never committed wrongdoing. The "no regrets" proclaimer might go an extra step. In a belief that good things always come from bad, the "no regrets" person might feel no need to wish that events had gone any other way. Maybe whatever happened was for the best.

The "greater good" hypothesis can relieve them of the painful feeling of regret. Of course, morally this is awful logic to live by. I understand the psychological appeal, though. Declaring "no regrets" can make us feel that we are properly managing our emotional lives. Who wants to feel awful or pestered by events of the past? It's better to show psychic resilience. It can also make us feel that we have some type of control. After we've acted "out of control" via wrongdoing, regaining power over our minds is a first step, or that is the thought. Control is good to have, all things considered. But having good values (and signaling them) is better.

Regret and remorse can be agonizing. Their purpose is not to make us suffer. "The purpose of remorse is not the self-punishment, even if that is an effect," says Card. Rather, the "point is to not let us forget or lose the appreciation of what we did."[34] Contrary to self-alienation—which keeps us in the past—regret reminds us of the past so that we might learn from it, respond to it, and be a better person as a result. As the author Daniel H. Pink puts it: "Regrets reveal a need and yield a lesson. With moral regrets, the need is goodness. The lesson . . . is this: when in doubt, do the right thing."[35]

The challenge is finding a way to live with the pain, to accept the intrusive memories when they seem uncontrollable.[36] This is not easy. But it's much more difficult without self-forgiveness. A fictional illustration of this appears in the 2008 film *Seven Pounds*. The aeronautical engineer Tim Thomas cannot forgive himself for having caused a terrible car crash because he was texting while driving. His wife and six others died as a result. The accident leads Tim to atone for his actions by donating his organs to seven morally good people; eventually killing himself in order to make the last donation. Film critic Omer Mozaffar describes the movie as depicting "the caustic cruelty of remorse."[37] Mozaffar is correct in his description of remorse when he writes: "You see a tree or smell a scent or hear a voice, and you are triggered. Your memory carries you momentarily into the past . . . remorse is one of those feelings that keeps coming back to strangle us with the past." And I agree with him in part when he likens remorse to "a vicious debt collector that knocks on the door to my heart on its own erratic schedule." Yet I disagree with Mozaffar's depiction of remorse as vicious and cruel. Remorse is vicious and cruel for Tim only because he has not forgiven himself. He has not let go of self-contempt, self-hatred, and resentment. Tim's remorse is controlling him because he has not gotten any relief or release via forgiveness. He can't live with himself, therefore, he can't live with remorse. It needn't be this way.

I cannot promise you that self-forgiveness will make regret less painful. But I believe that it can help make it less destructive, allowing you to live with yourself and the past, despite the pain. This is what repair is all about.

10

RADICAL REPAIR

WITH OR WITHOUT FORGIVENESS

WHILE EVERYONE was making bread during the coronavirus pandemic lockdown, I was discovering a different kind of hobby: Formula One Racing. The sport is not as popular in America as it is in other parts of the world, so I didn't pay much attention to it until 2020. But once I was introduced to the motorsport through the magic of a social media algorithm, I was hooked.

Hobbies invite nerd-dom. Some might say they require it. Plus, I am obsessive by nature. I wasn't content with merely waking up before sunrise to watch a Sunday Grand Prix. I wanted to learn everything I could about the sport. I needed to know how the cars worked, the nature of the teamwork involved, the skills required of drivers, as well as the out-of-this-world logistics needed to organize biweekly races in different countries around the world. I would have never suspected, however, that this inquiry would also help me understand interpersonal repair more deeply.

Before each race, the ten teams participate in practice sessions. The purpose of a session is to allow the drivers to adjust to the track and external conditions, and to make sure their cars are running well for race day. If there are problems with the cars, the engineers in the garage get to work. If there are any crashes during the practice or qualifying sessions, workers in the garage (in collaboration with those in the home factory) have only a few hours to repair the cars for Sunday's race. In addition to repairing the cars when they break down, the engineers and mechanics also perform maintenance on the cars, both between and during the races.

Oh, and it's called *Formula* One for a reason. Not all F1 teams' power units are on a par. The cars might look alike, but there are important differences under the hood. This is because every few years, or "eras," the International Automobile Federation lays out new rules and regulations that cars and drivers must follow. And each team—through innovation and ingenuity—creates a power unit that can succeed given these specifications. Teams that create the best power units are usually at the top of the grid and consistently on the winning podium. Currently, the three teams are Mercedes, Ferrari, and Red Bull. But who knows if this will last when the federation provides new specifications.

Formula One's cycle of innovation, maintenance, and mending reminds me of what's required in our own lives and relationships. Let's call this cycle *radical repair*. On our own tracks of life, we are striving to succeed but often crash, hurt ourselves and others, and fail to make proper adjustments. When this happens, we need radical repair.

There are several senses in which we use the word "radical" in English. "Radical" comes from the Latin word meaning "having roots," which explains why "radical leaves" refer to leaves that grow at the root and "radical surgery" refers to surgery that aims to correct the fundamental problem. Then there's radical in the sense of progressive or extreme, which suggests that one is aiming for complete change or deviation from the norm. For these reasons, Martin Luther King Jr. was considered a radical when Jim Crow reigned supreme; and women suffragists were described as radical for their uncivil disobedience to win the vote for women. And then there's the surfer's truncated version of the word, "rad," which means excellence. Added together, the phrase "radical repair"—as I use it—refers to repair that involves addressing the root of a problem, aiming for change, and engaging in excellent teamwork.

F1 is a sport that employs radical repair. Teams can't have lemons on the track, so experts are needed to address and fix the root of any car problem that arises. During each race, drivers and engineers make technical adjustments to help the car perform better than it did in the previous race. But to succeed, everyone must do their part. No matter how brilliantly the race is going, a pit crew taking a few seconds too long to change the tires can make the difference between winning a race and coming in seventh.

Similarly, both we and our relationships are in constant need of radical repair—repair that gets at the root, makes the necessary adjustments, and is collaborative. It's a repair in which relief, release, and reconciliation feature prominently. In this chapter I'll shed more light on radical repair, its relationship to forgiveness, and the necessity of attempting it—even if, in the end, it's not fully within our grasp.

GETTING AT THE ROOT

Throughout this book I have contrasted the worthy aims of forgiveness with what I have referred to as superficial repair. To better understand what radical repair requires, and why we need it, it will be beneficial to explain why superficial repair (and its close cousin, thrifty repair) are inadequate to achieve the moral goods of forgiveness.

Superficial repair is repair in appearance only. A person might request forgiveness without any real concern that the relationship has healed. A spouse, for instance, might ask their partner to forgive them without attending to the persisting anger or hurt. They merely hope their spouse will act as if everything is OK, even if it no longer is. Or a political leader might ask a racial minority community to forgive, with the hope that their granting of forgiveness would communicate to the public that they can move on from the historical mistreatment—even if reparations are lacking, continual resentment remains, or present-day oppression has yet to be addressed. In both examples, the requesters are hoping that the forgiveness would produce superficial repair.

This kind of repair aims at appearance in two senses. In one sense, its *literal appearance*—how it looks from the outside. It's like opting for body work over engine work. People who aim or settle for superficial repair are more concerned with how the relationship looks than whether it actually works. They prefer a shallow, surface-level fix than the deeper, necessary repair.

In another sense of appearance, superficial repair is concerned with *temporary fixes*. We might constantly refill our car with motor oil so that the oil light will disappear. But we never give it an oil change. Or our mechanic might decide to sculpt our brake pads instead of replacing them. The real problem might look like it's been addressed: the oil light disappears; the brakes stop grinding. But all of this is temporary. Soon the oil light reappears. After a few months, we start to hear grinding sounds each time we stop at a light. Because we haven't attended to the underlying issue, the problem quickly creeps back up, revealing itself.

What might this look like in a relationship? A couple might forgive each other in order to change the way they talk to each other. Doing so may repair the way they express their problems—perhaps the tone of their complaints is less hostile—but the underlying reasons for the complaints (e.g., hurt, disappointment, or repeated offenses) remain unaddressed. A couple could also forgive to restore honesty. But if they do not try to fix the initial source of the dishonesty (such as unhappiness or infidelity), they are likely to continue to have problems in the relationship. In these two instances, it seems that the couple is achieving repair via forgiveness. However, because the repairs are temporary fixes that do not address the underlying issue, problems and ruptures will continue to creep up.

In addition to superficial repair, there is what I call *thrifty repair*. This involves fixing only what is least costly or more likely to bring us comfort. This often comes at the neglect of the difficult, yet necessary-to-attend-to ruptures. When it comes to cars, we might fix the window but not the transmission because window repair is cheaper. Or we might fix the air conditioner but not the brake lights because the former will make driving more comfortable.[1] We pay little concern to fixing the most pressing problem. What matter most is cost and comfort. Thrifty repair can also occur by using cheap parts—parts that will quickly deteriorate, requiring their own repair.

A small community aims, or settles, for thrifty repair when they refuse to pay the cost for deep repair. They decline to hold wrongdoers accountable, refrain from listening to all victims, or fail to implement compensatory measures. They might think that the victim's forgiveness is all that is needed to bring about repair, without accepting the true costs. And because members are unwilling to accept and do what's required of them, they neglect important areas—deciding only to fix that which does not

require much from them. When addressing the hate-based violence that's been happening in their neighborhood, they might
try to adopt policies that will halt violence, or at least make it less
likely. These policies will not focus, however, on fixing the cause
of the violence, getting at the root. And that's because addressing the manifestation of violence is the least costly fix.
Addressing hate and other negative attitudes and perceptions in
the community is more difficult and uncomfortable.

Radical repair is different from superficial and thrifty repair
in every regard. Radical repair attempts to get at the root of the
problem, no matter the cost. It's about fixing what's actually
broken, rather than opting for cosmetic repairs. It doesn't focus
merely on the symptoms, but on the cause.

In a case of a cheating spouse, the aim is not just to repair
their relationship, which would require restoring trust, recom-
mitting, and so on. Doing so is, of course, important. But the
cheating spouse would also attempt to get at the root of the
infidelity. More than likely, they would need to repair themselves too. Perhaps they will have to address and fix the psychological issues and moral flaws that led to their infidelity, such as
vulnerability, a weak ego, low self-esteem, or selfishness. In the
case of the neighborhood plagued by hate-based violence, radical repair would involve repairing the hateful attitudes and
emotions of individual members and dismantling the exclusionary activities and institutions within the community. It cannot occur by only ending violence.

Those who engage in radical repair embrace discomfort. It's
likely to feel uncomfortable to acknowledge that violating a
partner's trust was the result of selfishness rather than the
simple, sexist excuse that "boys will be boys!" It's uncomfortable to admit that hate-based violence taking place in one's
community is not simply the result of a few bad eggs, but is

instead the result of community members' complicity and inaction when, for example, they allowed neighbors to perpetuate hateful stereotypes in Homeowners Association meetings and display hateful signs in their yards. Addressing this past behavior may cause the community embarrassment and require difficult confrontation. But this is the cost they must pay if they want radical repair. Engaging in radical repair is acknowledging that if anything is to be truly fixed, *we* are likely to have a role to play and a price to pay.

Formula One is a billion-dollar industry. Teams with the highest budgets are typically those who finish at the top of the grid each year. With more money, teams are able to pay top drivers, hire competent leadership and engineers, engage in top innovation. And this shows on the track. It costs to win in the sport. Heck, it costs to attempt to win. And it's not just the teams who bear a cost. The drivers do too. They can lose five to ten pounds in sweat per race because of the extreme temperatures they endure while racing. Radical repair similarly requires sacrifice from all parties involved. Victims must be willing to absorb some pain; wrongdoers must be willing to be vulnerable or compensate victims; communities must be willing to demand justice and vindicate victims.[2] This is what radical repair entails.

Often, radical repair requires time. For instance, it takes time to restore trust after infidelity; to feel vulnerable with those who once took your kindness for weakness; to feel safe around those who turned a blind eye to your mistreatment or refused to come to your defense.

This is not to say that we can repair anything if we just give it time. The philosopher Margaret Walker powerfully reminds us that some people who undergo awful situations "are not simply healed by time even when they are able to reclaim their lives," and that "some hearts broken by betrayal or cruelty never mend."[3] Some breaks are irreparable, and some people, despite their best efforts, may carry their brokenness with them for a lifetime. Nor is this to say that every relationship is worth repairing. In her book *Repair*, the philosopher Elizabeth Spelman contends that there is nothing sacred about a previous state or relationship to suggest that we should always aim to return there through reparative endeavors.[4] While it may be worth the effort to restore a classic Porsche, we have little reason to make the effort to restore Ford Pintos, which were unsafe and discontinued owing to the location of their fuel tanks. Some things and some relationships, because of the danger they pose, should not be repaired or restored.

The Pinto is also an example of the dangers of thrifty repair. When the issue with the fuel tank came to light, Ford estimated that it would be cheaper to pay lawsuits than fix the problem. They were unwilling to bear the cost of fixing the underlying problem. They decided it was cheaper to fix their bottom line than repair their cars. But someone paid the cost: customers lost their lives, and those who survived accidents were badly burned.[5]

Superficial repair is no repair at all. It is not only a shallow and cheap way to respond to problems. Repairing moral ruptures and preventing new ones require us to fix the root of our problems—despite the cost and discomfort.

NO "I" IN TEAMWORK

One of the most frequent questions asked after a driver wins the Formula One World Championship is "Is it the driver or the car?" Are race car drivers successful because they have the best car? Or are they successful because they are the best driver? When Mercedes driver Sir Lewis Hamilton won his seventh world title in the 2020 season, many thought the answer was clear, and credited his impeccable handling and track mastery for the victory.

We can ask a similar question in the aftermath of wrongdoing. Who should we credit for the success of radical repair: the victim or the wrongdoer? Often we think there is only one answer. And that answer is usually the victim. However, if there is any possibility for radical repair, it will never come about because of the work of one person. As much as Hamilton has shown that he is a skillful driver, his wins are not the result of that alone. He also wins because of the engineers, the pit crew, the decisions of leadership, and the support of family and friends. When he won his ninety-second race, becoming the most successful driver in F1 history, Hamilton, with tears in his eyes and humility in his voice, said, "Such an honor to work with you [the Mercedes Team]." After the race he told a reporter, "I really owe it all to these guys for their teamwork, continually innovating and pushing the barrier ever higher every year."[6]

In our interpersonal lives, engagement in and success at radical repair relies not on one individual but on all relevant parties. And the relevant parties are not just victims or wrongdoers. They also include our respective communities at home, at work, or online. Yes, wrongdoers are part of our communities. And they too have a reparative role to play in radical repair. They should do their best to make amends by taking responsibility for their actions, sincerely apologizing, and, in some cases, taking compensatory measures. However, communities also have a role to play.

We've seen how important communities are in the workplace post-conflict, and in the context of transitional justice, such as post-apartheid South Africa. But more can be said about their role. One of the roles of communities, according to Margaret

Walker, is to demand and support repair.[7] Social services, courts, and nonprofit organizations can support repair. Social services can provide psychological and economic resources post-conflict. Courts can demand accountability, providing relief for victims. Nonprofit organizations can provide educational and mediation support. But communities can also provide voice, validation, and vindication.[8]

Communities give voice to victims when they listen to their testimonies. As Walker writes, "Being willing to hear victims is already validating, and sometimes the ability to tell or to have wrong acknowledged by others is vindicating."[9] When our community acknowledges our claims and responds to them, they recognize us as community members. In essence, they tell us, "We see you." When they fail to give us voice or listen to our reports of wrongdoing, this not only leaves our present wounds exposed, but creates new wounds, as we are deprived by our community of the support we need. Walker suggests that "if the community . . . ignores the victim, challenges the victim's credibility, treats the victim's complaint as of little import, shelters or sides with the perpetrators of wrong, or worse, overtly or by implication blames the victim, the victim will feel abandoned and isolated."[10] Radical repair is less likely to happen when this occurs.

Listening and validating are often easier said than done. As the philosophers Kristie Dotson, Cassie Herbert, and Kate Abramson have pointed out, we often do an injustice to others when they report wrongdoing to us.[11] We might engage in what they call "testimonial injustice" by failing to give victims credibility because of their gender, race, or class. We doubt what they report, not because we detect falsehood, but simply because we are conditioned to provide certain speakers with less credibility than others. When a poor Hispanic woman reports that her male boss sexually harassed her, we may doubt her report, not based on any judgment about the evidence, but because of the roles and identities of the two parties. We might also engage in gaslighting by emotionally manipulating victims into thinking that their perception of wrongful events is mistaken and baseless, or morally wrong. We might deny that our favorite neighbor called someone a slur because, well, we know him. Perhaps the reporter of the slur is so sensitive or crazy that they heard something that wasn't actually uttered. These responses are more likely to occur in instances in which community members engage in "risky speech"—speech that challenges power structures—such as reports of sexual violence (which challenges misogyny and rape culture) and racism (which challenges racial hierarchies and white supremacy). People who report these incidents are often met with disbelief (or worse). But such responses block or delay radical repair. For how can we take part in repair when we fail to acknowledge that a rupture has occurred and someone has been harmed?

These responses can also cause new wounds. When we fail to acknowledge a person's victimhood and deny them credibility, we violate their trust and abandon the communal responsibilities we have to each other, creating more anger, despair, terror.[12] To escape these harms, communities should understand that one of their most important roles in radical repair is to listen to, validate, and vindicate victims—and to do this regardless of whether the victim is willing to forgive.

Communities also have the important role of reminding each other of the group's standards for how they should treat each other. When a person violates these standards, we should rebuke and reprove them to remind them and other members of our shared moral values and principles. When we do this, it communicates that we take wrongdoing seriously. It communicates that—as my mother often reminded my sister and me—"in our house, that's not what we do." In our community, we do not mistreat women. In our community, we do not take what is not ours to take. In our neighborhood, we provide safety to vulnerable members. By reminding each other of these standards and holding ourselves accountable when we violate them, we also communicate that there are consequences for not adhering to them.[13] Reiterating these standards can also serve to acknowledge victims, because it communicates that victims are under the communities' covering. This aids in radical repair.

The possibility for radical repair cannot happen simply because a victim has forgiven or a wrongdoer has apologized. Radical repair requires collaboration. We tend to underemphasize the important role communities play in the work of repair. Like the largely anonymous pit crews that make victory possible for their teams' famous drivers, community members make radical repair possible. And when our communities underperform by responding slowly to wrongdoing, failing to take problems seriously, or refusing to hold each other accountable, not only can they inhibit radical repair, they can create new problems and harms that require our attention.

INNOVATE! INNOVATE! INNOVATE!

As I noted earlier, racing teams must innovate in preparation for new eras. A failure to innovate often translates to a failure to compete. It's easy to think that innovation occurs only behind the scenes, at the home factory, with a look to the future. But innovation also occurs during the season, on the track, and in the garage. Teams must come up with strategies for each race based on track and weather conditions. They also must adapt their strategies considering grid positioning, accidents, and pit crew mishaps. Innovation is constantly happening.

Radical repair in our human lives and relationships also involves innovation and creativity—and is not simply a matter of putting things back to the way they once were. As Elizabeth Spelman reminds us, repair involves "something distinctly different from the original creation . . . but also [something distinctly different] from its accidental or deliberate destruction, its abandonment."[14] Radical repair brings about a new state—different from both creation and destruction—which we can only reach with human ingenuity and creative adaptation.

Why do we need creativity to repair ourselves and our relationships? I propose two reasons. First, our reparative toolkit contains a variety of tools—such as forgiveness, validation, justice, mediation, and economic and psychological support— and we must know which tool, or combination of tools, will fix the problem. As any episode of The Food Network's Chopped will prove, the ability to work with a limited set of ingredients is an act of ingenuity. Similarly, knowing what to do with a set of reparative tools is a creative endeavor. We tend to think that forgiveness is the only tool that can fix our problems, yet forgiveness alone will often be insufficient to bring about repair. We may need validation and vindication from the community in combination with our forgiveness. Or we may find that forgiveness won't do the job of fixing our racial crisis, and the tools we need are apologies, justice, and reparations.

Radical repair also involves creativity through its use of strategy. It may require going against conventional thinking and trying new plans when the old ones no longer work. The conventional thinking about repairing a marriage is that the spouses should go to counseling. Conventional thinking for repairing a sibling rivalry is to hug it out. But these strategies may not fit your situation, or the character or disposition of the people involved, so radical repair will require creative thinking.

Being creative might require the couple to admit that because they are reticent around strangers, counseling is not the right solution for them. Perhaps they need daily meetings to talk things out with each other. Or a society might recognize, as South Africa did, that while retributive justice may have worked for other societies, it will not work for them. The South African context requires something different, something more like amnesty and truth commissions to usher in repair. This is creative thinking. A company might come to realize that while sending feuding co-workers to Human Resources or promoting a culture of forgiveness worked when the company was a startup, the expansion of the company may require new approaches to deal with conflict. Radical repair requires experimentation and recognizing what no longer works. In an earlier cultural moment, a celebrity could simply issue a public apology to repair their relationship with fans. But this may no longer be sufficient. Today, a celebrity may need to redo a song, donate money to a cause, educate themselves, or seek out psychological help. Radical repair requires that we recognize that—no matter how discomforting—we may have to do things differently in order to get different reparative results.

Sometimes the most creative thing we can do is to recognize and admit that something cannot be repaired. As strange as this might sound, despite the wealth and ingenuity of Formula One, not everything on an F1 car can be repaired. Pit crews replace worn tires (instead of repairing them) up to three times during a race. The word "repair" misleadingly implies, as Walker points out, that "a broken moral relationship can be fixed, and that when fixed it will be fully or largely restored, [become] 'good as new.'" In some ways, I am guilty of misleading you with my use of the phrase "radical repair," given this implication.

Such restoration, or "good as new" repair, can happen. A small rupture between best friends could make them even closer and stronger. But if the injury is more severe, it might be impossible for them to continue as friends. Some injuries are just irreparable. We should recognize when something cannot be fixed, no matter how hard we try. This doesn't mean that we were unwilling or weren't creative. It simply means that not everything can be repaired. One of the most creative insights is recognizing this fact.

This doesn't mean that we should not engage in any reparative activities. You don't know if something can be fixed until you try. But relationships are not the only targets of radical repair. When it comes to repairing ourselves, getting as close to wholeness as we can is an achievement—even if we remain broken. In this way, we become like Kintsugi—the Japanese art of mending broken pieces of pottery with powdered metals. The brokenness and attempt at repair are not hidden from view but become a visible part of the pottery's history. A certain beauty results despite the imperfection of having been repaired. Therefore, engaging in radical repair is never a waste of time.

GIVING IN TO OUR INSTINCTS

We often refer to our species as *Homo sapiens*. But Spelman challenges us to see ourselves also as *Homo reparans*, a species equipped with a *reparative instinct*. The evidence is overwhelming. We don't just fix cars; we mend clothing, repair buildings, and rebuild reputations. We don't settle for damage or accept that things can't be put back together, so we engage in a variety of reparative activities. Because we are fragile and our relationships are subject to fraying, we too are an object of repair. Our appetite for fixing is voracious. And it pleases us to be able to repair things. But there is another "instinctive" option on the table.

The psychologist Michael McCullough thinks we have a *forgiveness instinct*. McCullough believes we developed this instinct because it helps repair and preserve the valuable relationships that we depend on for our survival. A variety of evolutionary and psychological evidence supports this view. The hypothesis aligns with the fact that we often forgive in order to get the benefits of cooperation; that we are social animals who depend on each other for survival; and that forgiveness is more common among close relatives and friends on whom we heavily depend. McCullough contends, "Natural selection seems to have outfitted us with a forgiveness instinct because it helped our ancestors preserve relationships that have biological utility."[15] Improving our survival and maintaining valuable cooperative relationships are the "ultimate causes of desire to forgive and reconcile."[16]

In my view, we should think of the reparative instinct as the more basic of the two, with the forgiveness instinct understood as one manifestation of our more general instinct to repair. The forgiveness instinct is more likely to arise in the context of close relationships that we want reconciled. As I've argued throughout this book, there are other aims in the aftermath of wrongdoing besides reconciliation. There are times when we cannot reconcile our relationships, such as when a previous relationship was inadequate. Nevertheless, the reparative instinct is still at work. It's best to say, then, that we have a reparative instinct in general. In certain contexts, we may have a drive to forgive. This drive is an outgrowth of the reparative instinct we all have. We forgive for reparative reasons.

And even when we can't or don't desire to reconcile our valuable relationships, the reparative instinct remains. In these contexts, we are still trying to figure out how to fix our lives, mend our hearts, restore our relations. Why does this matter? Well, there are moments when you don't feel like forgiving—which, as I've argued, is often justified. What I hope we humans maintain, though—even in the absence of the forgiveness drive—is a *reparative instinct*. The instinct to forgive may be absent in certain contexts, irrelevant for certain relationships, and misused and abused. But if we stay committed to radical repair, with all that it involves, then we will always be better equipped to make sure that damage doesn't have the last word, ruptures don't get worse, and we are responding productively to our fragility. My hope is that we do what we can to ensure that our reparative instinct remains radical through it all.

CONCLUSION

DOING FORGIVENESS BETTER

ON JULY 24, 2022, Pope Francis arrived in Canada to take part in a weeklong tour to ask for forgiveness from Indigenous groups. He took the trip in order to try to make amends, given the needs expressed by Indigenous groups after the recent discovery of unmarked graves at former residential schools, a high percentage of which had been run by the Catholic Church, that operated from 1870 to 1996 with the mission of assimilating more than 150,000 Indigenous children. What happened at those schools was far more sinister. Several priests and nuns beat children for speaking their native language, sexually abused them, and starved some children to death. The pope, speaking to Indigenous groups that included survivors and their families, asked for forgiveness. However, his requests lacked specificity and reparative commitments. Over several days, he expressed the following:

> With shame and unambiguously, I humbly beg forgiveness for the evil committed by so many Christians against the Indigenous people.[1]

I want to tell you how very sorry I am and to ask for forgiveness for the evil perpetrated by not [a] few Catholics who contributed to the policies of cultural assimilation and enfranchisement in those schools.[2]

I ask forgiveness, in particular, for the ways in which many members of the Church and of religious communities cooperated, not least through their indifference, in projects of cultural destruction and forced assimilation promoted by the government of that time, which culminated in the system of residential schools.[3]

Some people in the crowd wept; others applauded when Pope Francis apologized and condemned the policy of assimilation. However, some survivors were critical of Pope Francis. For them the apology and requests for forgiveness fell short of what they had hoped from the pope. They criticized the pope for his failure to specify the nature of the crimes. Ruth Roulette hoped "he would be more specific in his apology," noting that the pope failed to mention sexual abuse. One person screamed from the audience, demanding that the pope mention the fifteenth-century doctrine that justified the taking of Indigenous land. Others criticized the pope for failing to propose or commit to any reparative action. Addressing this need, Henry Pitawanakwat, whose mother was a survivor, said, "An apology doesn't mean anything to me. It's just another word in the English language unless it is supported by some kind of action, such as funding to help us support our language and culture."[4] Jack Anawak, an Inuit leader, admitted, "Their load will lighten (after the apology) but the trauma they feel will still be there and they'll need help." Both Pitawanakwat and Anawak urged the church to provide more money to support survivors and the community. The Catholic Church, however, did not mention either compensation or justice-related aims.

For example, Natan Obed, the president of an Inuit-serving nonprofit organization, said that the pope did not respond to his request to make a plea to France to extradite a retired priest charged with sexual assault. "The Pope himself has not responded to any of the requests we have made, although, he looked sympathetic. . . . We have asked multiple times and the request[s] were made . . . today. No resolution to date."[5] Wallace Yellowface, a seventy-eight-year-old survivor, believed that the apology came too late. He expressed doubt that the apology would do any good, and he said he was still trying to figure out what happened to his missing sister, who had been sent to one of the schools.

Herein lies an example of what I have referred to as failures of forgiveness. While there is nothing wrong with apologizing and asking for forgiveness, the critics of the pope say that he failed in his role as a requester. He did not present conditions (for example, reparation and justice) that would make it more likely that the survivors would forgive the Church—making us wonder if he was after superficial rather than radical repair. The pope's apology, while not so quick as the hurry-and-bury ritual, was too late and therefore ineffective at best and problematic at worst. We need to remember that forgiveness can help us mend our wounds, but how we practice it as requesters, extenders, withholders, critics, and bystanders can have a tremendous impact on its healing potential.

This is not to suggest that we need to practice "perfect forgiveness." There is no such thing, and this is why I have promoted the concept of "imperfect forgiveness" throughout this book. The idea of imperfect forgiveness is that forgiveness does not take place in ideal conditions or create ideal outcomes. I might forgive even though I have not received an apology. You might forgive and still be unable to find relief. Pope Francis might offer a specific apology, compensation, and justice-related acts, yet there is no guarantee that all survivors would then be able to forgive, even if they tried. Nonetheless, just because forgiveness is imperfect doesn't mean that we shouldn't try our best to do forgiveness better.

My aim in this book has been to get us to rethink forgiveness with the hopes that it would improve our expectations and our behavior. If I have been successful at all, you will be equipped and even motivated to think, expect, and behave better—whatever your role may be in the aftermath of wrongdoing.

There are several ways we can live up to the challenge of doing forgiveness better. I've noted that we can think better about forgiveness by reconceiving it not as one thing or as aspiring toward one goal. Instead we should think of it as a set of practices that might aim at several reparative aims. We should also rethink who plays a part in forgiveness. It's never just the victim. We all have a role to play, and I have challenged us to be careful in our roles by noting what we should and shouldn't do and why—such as refraining from demanding forgiveness, because such demands disrespect victims' right to make their own decisions. I've also offered ways to escape certain dangers—such as forgiving when we are not ready to, all because we think that opting for revenge is the opposite of forgiveness. Thinking better about forgiveness also involves rejecting the idea that forgiveness is "the" solution to our problems. After forgiveness, we may have to do more. We might have to offer reparations, fire an employee, cut off a family member, cancel a celebrity, continue therapy, or live with regret. This shows that forgiveness alone is not enough to curb conflict, and that in some instances forgiveness alone cannot fully repair communities and ourselves.

Thinking better about forgiveness also includes broadening our view of forgiveness, which will help us see better. It will help us see forgiveness where we thought it was absent. It will prevent us from engaging in the process problem and the protection problem with our families. It will, instead, enable us to make room for our loved one's anger and begin to care, listen, and decenter ourselves.

We can also expect better from ourselves. As community members we have an obligation to validate victims and to stand by and enforce the moral standards of our communities. Radical repair requires this kind of teamwork. We must refrain from asking victims whether they will forgive and instead ask them what we can do for them.

We can also lower our expectations about forgiveness and repair. After forgiveness, our relationships might never go back to the way they once were. We might face deep remorse after we forgive ourselves. This doesn't mean that our efforts at forgiveness were pointless.

We can also behave better. This involves being patient with victims, refraining from rushing them to forgive, and being empathetic instead. We can also refrain from accusing extenders of forgiveness of forgiving too quickly. We should trust that they know when it is the right time to begin their forgiveness journey. We must make sure that we are not interpreting people's forgiveness as sending bad social messages, remembering that their aims may outweigh these messages. We can also do better when accessing withholders. Just because they haven't forgiven doesn't mean they don't desire repair. Forgiveness is one way toward repair but not the only way. Withholders, like Zeneta Everhart—whose son was injured in the 2022 racist mass shooting in Buffalo, New York—can engage in praiseworthy behavior. While standing before the murderer at his sentencing, she declared: "The world says you have to forgive in order to move on. But I stand before you today to say that will never happen."[6] We should recognize withholders' courage and generosity rather than ignore it.

We must be diligent in making sure we do not pressure or coerce victims to forgive—let alone pressure them so that we ourselves might feel better and less uncomfortable. Forgiveness is not a moral duty. It is a gift that victims share with us. Behaving better also means ensuring that we do not misuse forgiveness for unethical or illegal purposes. We should create a culture at work that makes forgiveness possible rather than use it to obscure sexual assault, harassment, and racism. Because forgiveness is not the only solution to conflicts at work, we should be open to and creative with other coping strategies. Behaving better requires that we request forgiveness only when we have the standing, and that we only make requests that are appropriate and empowering, rather than disrespectful and insensitive.

When it comes to self-forgiveness, we must be neither too hard nor too easy on ourselves. We must try to stay clear of shame, self-alienation, and irrational self-reproach, which only keep us in the past and in hiding. We must use our own guilt as motivation to make amends and be better.

Improving our thinking, expectations, and behavior around forgiveness will radically change the way we respond to conflict and wrongdoing in our lives. The good news is that we only have to learn to do forgiveness better, not perfectly. When we do, rewards await.

ACKNOWLEDGMENTS

IT TAKES A VILLAGE to write a book. I am proud to say that I have the most brilliant, supportive, and loving village on planet Earth.

I began thinking about forgiveness in graduate school. I was lucky to have an advisor—Samuel Fleischacker—who was open to me working on forgiveness in a way that was, let's say, "atypical." He challenged me every step of the way, and helped me become a better philosopher. I am also grateful to other graduate school advisors—Anthony Laden, Anne Eaton, Alice MacLachlan, and Charles Mills—for their support and insightful feedback in developing lots of the ideas that are in this book. Charles Mills's passing in 2021 has left a huge hole in my heart and in our philosophy community. I hope this book makes him proud.

I would also like to thank Tommie Shelby for his feedback on early drafts of several chapters of this work, as well as my fellowship cohorts at the Edmond J. Safra Center for Ethics and the Hutchins Center for African and African American Research at Harvard University.

My literary agent–Margo Fleming–believes in me till no end. How did I get so lucky? (It's for this reason that she will always be "Special Agent Margo.") My editorial team was a joy to work with. I am thankful to my editor Rob Tempio for his enthusiasm for this project. Much appreciation to Amanda Moon, Thomas

LeBien, and James Brandt at Moon & Company for helping this verbose philosopher write better prose.

I have benefited immensely from questions and criticisms from audiences at Boston University, MIT, Brooklyn College, the University of Witwatersrand at Johannesburg, Harvard University, the University of Washington at St. Louis, and the University of Michigan.

Thanks to Cassie Herbert, Luvell Anderson, Mafaz Al-Suwaidan, Lynne Tirrell, Christopher Lewis, Flip Tanedo, Matthew King, Lucy Allias, Kathryn Norlock, Brandon Terry, Charles Griswold, Axelle Karera, Kris Sealey, Jason Reynolds, Lidal Dror, Christine Platt, and others for their fruitful suggestions and constant encouragement.

NOTES

CHAPTER 1: WHAT TO EXPECT WHEN YOU ARE EXPECTING FORGIVENESS

1. Katherine Schwarzenegger Pratt, *The Gift of Forgiveness: Inspiring Stories from Those Who Have Overcome the Unforgivable* (New York: Penguin Books, 2021). The prevalence of the narrow view of forgiveness can be seen in the publisher's description of the book: "A fresh, inspiring book on learning how to forgive—with firsthand stories from those who have learned to let go of resentment and find peace."

2. Schwarzenegger Pratt, *The Gift of Forgiveness,* 104.

3. Andrea Tornielli, "Gun Shots, Fear, Prayer and Forgiveness," *Vatican News,* May 14, 2021, https://www.vaticannews.va/en/pope/news/2021-05/gun-shots-fear -prayer-and-forgiveness.html.

4. Al Hunter, "Dr. Martin Luther King, Jr. in Indianapolis, Part 2," *Weekly View,* June 9, 2014, http://weeklyview.net/2014/01/09/dr-martin-luther-king-jr-in-indiana polis-part-2/.

5. Jeffrie G. Murphy, *Getting Even: Forgiveness and Its Limits* (New York: Oxford University Press, 2003), 77.

6. Macalester Bell, *Hard Feelings: The Moral Psychology of Contempt* (New York: Oxford University Press, 2013), 8.

7. Jean Hampton, "Forgiveness, Resentment, and Hatred," in *Forgiveness and Mercy,* ed. Jeffrie G. Murphy and Jean Hampton (Cambridge: Cambridge University Press, 1988).

8. Hampton, "Forgiveness, Resentment, and Hatred," 83.

9. Kathryn Norlock, in a new preface to her *Forgiveness from a Feminist Perspective* (Lanham, MD: Lexington Books, 2009), is right to point to the fact that broader conceptions are increasingly becoming the norm instead of the exception in the philosophical literature, but it has taken a while for this narrow view to be challenged outside of academia.

10. In the United States, the phrase colloquially means "Has the problem been resolved?" or "Is the relationship OK?"

11. Other philosophers who hold a broad conception include Norlock, *Forgiveness from a Feminist Perspective*.

12. Alice MacLachlan, "Practicing Imperfect Forgiveness," in *Feminist Ethics and Social and Political Philosophy: Theorizing the Non-Ideal*, ed. Lisa Tessman (Dordrecht: Springer, 2009), 191.

13. Alice MacLachlan, "Authoritative Norms and Internal Goods: The Normativity of Moral Practices," manuscript (2015), 3.

14. To be sure, MacLachlan admits that the question of who has the standing is the most controversial norm.

CHAPTER 2: FORGIVERS AND WITHHOLDERS

1. "'I Don't Forgive This Woman, and She Needs Help': Black Child Wrongly Accused of Grabbing 'Cornerstore Caroline,'" ABC News, October 16, 2018, https://abcnews.go.com/US/white-woman-apologizes-alleging-black-child-assaulted-york/story?id=58505763.

2. Enjoli Francis and Bill Hutchinson, "'I Don't Forgive This Woman, and She Needs Help': Black Child Wrongly Accused of Grabbing 'Cornerstore Caroline,'" ABC News, October 16, 2018, https://abcnews.go.com/US/white-woman-apologizes-alleging-black-child-assaulted-york/story?id=58505763.

3. Martha Nussbaum makes this criticism in *Anger and Forgiveness* (New York: Oxford University Press, 2016), 75–85.

4. If this is right, then the critics have more work to do. They also have to convince me there is something wrong with the former.

5. I say more about this case in my essay "Racialized Forgiveness," *Hypatia: A Journal of Feminist Philosophy* 36, no. 4 (2021).

6. Chantal Da Silva, "'Forgiveness' Is Trending after Moment Botham Jean's Brother Hugged Police Officer Who Killed Him and Told Her: 'I Don't Even Want You to Go to Jail,'" Newsweek.com, October 3, 2019, https://www.newsweek.com/botham-jean-brother-bryant-offers-forgiveness-hug-amber-guyger-dallas-1462868.

7. Bill Chappell and Richard Gonzales, "Brandt Jean's Act of Grace toward His Brother's Killer Sparks a Debate over Forgiving," NPR, October 3, 2019, https://www.npr.org/2019/10/03/766866875/brandt-jeans-act-of-grace-toward-his-brother-s-killer-sparks-a-debate-over-forgi.

8. Ian Williamson, Marti Hope Gonzales, Sierra Fernandez, and Allison Williams, "Forgiveness Aversion: Developing a Motivational State Measure of Perceived Forgiveness Risks," *Motivation and Emotion* 38, no. 3 (2013): 380. doi:10.1007/s11031-013-9382-1.

9. Williamson et al., "Forgiveness Aversion," 381.

10. This would not count as forgiveness, because these are bodily practices rather than moral ones. I am not saying they are immoral. They are simply amoral practices that are essentially physical things we do. And we often do them without any thoughts about morality.

11. Darran Simon, Ed Lavandera, and Ashley Killough, "His Hug of Forgiveness Shocked the Country. Yet He Still Won't Watch the Video from That Moment," CNN .com, December 8, 2019, https://www.cnn.com/2019/12/06/us/brandt-jean -botham-jean-forgiveness/index.html.

12. It is my intention not to put these young men against each other. I am comparing them as opposed to contrasting. There is a difference.

CHAPTER 3: MAKING A GOOD ASK

1. I am *not* committed to a literal interpretation of these expressions or their literal forms. I understand that often when we say words, we do not always mean them literally. I think apologies and forgiveness requests may overlap in their usages. However, I am more concerned with what people may implicitly mean. I am also sensitive to the fact that what may sound like an apology can actually be a more polite way to request forgiveness. While I will be making use of specific forms of expressions in this chapter, I am not committed to their meaning the same thing in all contexts. I am also aware that people in other cultures may utter the same words and mean something different.

2. Charles Griswold, *Forgiveness: A Philosophical Exploration* (New York: Cambridge University Press, 2007); Jeffrie G. Murphy, *Getting Even: Forgiveness and Its Limits* (New York: Oxford University Press, 2003), 20.

3. Gary Chapman and Jennifer Thomas, *The Five Languages of Apology* (Chicago: Northfield, 2006), 101.

4. One might wonder whether it is wrong for a parent to tell a (young) child that he must forgive his sibling. Here I think the parent should command that the child *try* to forgive, or the parent should encourage forgiveness instead. But they should never command forgiveness. If anything, it's permissible for the parent to command that the child engage in a moral practice, such as "Don't take revenge on your sibling." But this is different from commanding forgiveness.

5. Thomas Nagel, in "Concealment and Exposure," *Philosophy and Public Affairs* 27, no. 1 (1998), writes: "We don't want to expose ourselves completely to strangers even if we don't fear their disapproval, hostility, or disgust. Naked exposure itself, whether or not it arouses disapproval, is disqualifying. The boundary between what we reveal and what we do not, and some control over that boundary, are among the most important attributes of our humanity" (17).

6. Consider Alisa L. Carse and Lynne Tirrell, "Forgiving Grave Wrongs," in *Forgiveness in Perspective*, ed. Christopher Allers and Marieke Smit (Amsterdam: Rodopi Press, 2010).

7. I am not arguing that this standard necessarily holds for victims. I argue that invitations should not be made without certain conditions being met, but I do not argue that victims should forgive or not forgive without certain met conditions.

8. This is always the case when third parties make requests. This might not always be the case with offenders, for they might apologize before the request. However, it is not the request that brings the offering, but the apology that follows.

9. Elizabeth Spelman, *Repair: The Impulse to Restore in a Fragile World* (Boston: Beacon Press, 2002).

10. Alice MacLachlan, "Gender and Public Apology," *Transitional Justice Review* 1, no. 2 (2013): 136–37.

11. MacLachlan, "Gender and Public Apology," 129–35.

12. Zenon Szablowinski, "Apology with and without a Request for Forgiveness," *Heythrop Journal* 53, no. 5 (2012): 731–41.

CHAPTER 4: FORGIVENESS AS POLITICAL PROJECT

1. There is disagreement about whether only interpersonal forgiveness, and not political forgiveness, is possible. Like MacLachlan ("The Philosophical Controversy over Political Forgiveness," in *Public Forgiveness in Post-Conflict Contexts*, ed. Paul van Tongeren, Neelke Doorn, and Bas van Stokkom [Cambridge: Intersentia, 2012]), I don't think political forgiveness contrasts with interpersonal relationships. We also have interpersonal relationships with our fellow citizens, although these may differ from our relationships with our family and friends. Political forgiveness emerges from our political relationships.

2. National Unity and Reconciliation Act, Section (3) (1), *Government Gazette* 361, no. 16579 (July 26, 1995).

3. To qualify, applicants had to have (1) committed a political crime (2) during 1960–1994 and (3) disclosed information about their crime. Applicants were not required to show remorse during the amnesty hearings, although a few of them did. Out of over 7,000 applications received, 2,328 applications received hearings and 568 applicants were granted amnesty. Seventy percent of applications came from those who were already imprisoned. See Richard A. Wilson, *The Politics of Truth and Reconciliation in South Africa: Legitimizing the Post-Apartheid State* (Cambridge: Cambridge University Press, 2001), 23.

4. Of the testifiers, 89.9 percent were African, 1.7 percent were Colored, and 1.1 percent were white.

5. Gross violations included the planning or committing of murders, abductions, torture, or severe ill-treatment.

6. Stéphane Leman-Langlois and Clifford D. Shearing, "Repairing the Future: The South African Truth and Reconciliation Commission at Work," in *Crime, Truth and Justice: Official Inquiry, Discourse, Knowledge*, ed. George Gilligan and John Pratt (Cullompton, UK: Willan, 2004), 211.

7. Committee members often possessed the victim's original statement during the hearing.

8. Leman-Langlois and Shearing, "Repairing the Future," 211.

9. Leman-Langlois and Shearing, "Repairing the Future," 211.

10. Ubuntu is a distinctively African value that means "people are people through other people." It means that people's humanity is bound up in others' humanity. Ubuntu emphasizes the priority of restorative justice and recognizes that vengeance and resentment can undermine harmony.

11. Linda Radzik and Colleen Murphy, "Reconciliation," in *Stanford Encyclopedia of Philosophy* (2015), https://plato.stanford.edu/search/searcher.py?query =reconciliation.

12. Wilson, *Politics of Truth and Reconciliation*, 174.

13. You will note that the following examples disproportionally involve women whose husbands or sons were the direct victims. This is not to suggest that women were not direct victims or perpetrators of crimes. The following explains the worry around women and their testimonies: "No questions about rape and gender-based violence were asked and if a woman spoke about being raped or experiencing gender-based violence, the statement-taker usually did not record it. When a woman insisted that their rape or gender violence be recorded in their statement, the statement-takers refused to record these incidents unless the woman had opened a case with the police. . . . The TRC processes did not view women as actors in the violence, but only as victims, and no women were cited as perpetrators of human rights violations even where women political prisoners recited violations committed against them by female prison warders" (Khulumani Support Group South Africa, "How the TRC Failed Women in South Africa: A Failure That Has Proved Fertile Ground for the Gender Violence Women in South Africa Face Today," October 3, 2011, http://www .khulumani.netitem/527-how-the-trc-failed-women-in-south-africa-a-failure-that -has-proved-fertile-ground-for-the-gender-violence-women-in-south-africa-face -today.htm). Recognizing this gap, and through the work and advocacy of women, the TRC established three separate Special Hearings on Women beginning in August 1996.

14. Truth and Reconciliation Commission, "Human Rights Violations, Submissions—Questions and Answers, Date: 12 May 1997, Name: Nomakhosazana Gladys Papu," http://www.justice.gov.za/trc/hrvtrans%5Ckwtown/papu.htm.

204 NOTES TO CHAPTER 4

15. Truth and Reconciliation Commission, "Human Rights Violations, Submissions—Questions and Answers, Date: 10th June 1997, Name: Mrs Bernice Elizabeth Whitefield," http://www.justice.gov.za/trc/hrvtrans%5Chrvel2/elnwhi .htm.

16. Truth and Reconciliation Commission, "Day 3—24 April 1996, Case No: CT/00205, Victim: Nomatise Evelyn Tsobileyo, Violation: Serious Injuries, Testimony from: Nomatise Evelyn Tsobileyo," http://www.justice.gov.za/trc /hrvtrans%5Cheide/ct00205.htm.

17. It should be noted that apologies as requests for forgiveness by perpetrators were rare. Only a few apologized during the amnesty hearings.

18. Desmond Tutu, *No Future without Forgiveness* (London: Random House, 1999), 271.

19. Ari Kohen, "The Person and the Political: Forgiveness and Reconciliation in Restorative Justice," *Critical Review of International Social and Political Philosophy* 12, no. 3 (2009): 404.

20. See Martha Minow, *Between Vengeance and Forgiveness: Facing History after Genocide and Mass Violence* (Boston: Beacon Press, 1998); and Kohen, "The Person and the Political."

21. My focus here is not necessarily on the benefits (healing) or disadvantages (for example, public shame in response to their answer) but on what the choosing was able to do. Also, these are only two examples of the ways in which victims could have asserted their autonomy. Other options might have included having a say in the prosecution of perpetrators. This varied. Some did have a say—particularly, for example, in the case of former South African Police colonel Eugene de Kock. Because amnesty, and not retribution, was on the table, the extent of this was limited.

22. Roger Friedman, "Widows to Testify at Hearings," Cape Times Independent Online, April 15, 1996, https://www.iol.co.za/.

23. Truth and Reconciliation Commission, *Truth and Reconciliation Commission of South Africa Report* (1998), 1:114, http://www.justice.gov.za/trc/report/finalreport /Volume%201.pdf.

24. Truth and Reconciliation Commission, *Report* (1998).

25. Wilson, in *Politics of Truth and Reconciliation*, claims that the TRC religious narrative put illiberal pressure on victims to forgive. Using the TRC as a primary example, Martha Minow claims that promoting forgiveness may jeopardize the rule of law. See Martha Minow, "Forgiveness, Law, and Justice," *California Law Review* 103, no. 6 (2015). Annelies Verdoolaege takes a careful look at the discourse used during the HRV hearings. She points out how some members of the committee put words into the mouths of testifiers; how the committee used the testifiers' original commitment to forgiveness and reconciliation as a way to make it difficult for testifiers to retract; and the difference in treatment of what she refers to as "ideal

testifiers" and "non-ideal testifiers." See Annelies Verdoolaege, *Reconciliation Discourse: The Case of the Truth and Reconciliation Commission*, vol. 27 of *Discourse Approaches to Politics, Society, and Culture* (Philadelphia: John Benjamins, 2008). Elizabeth Kiss is also concerned with how the TRC treated victims who dissented from forgiveness and reconciliation. It must be noted that most of the literature that supports or criticizes the TRC has focused on amnesty and justice and not forgiveness discourse. See Elizabeth Kiss, "Moral Ambition within and beyond Political Constraints," in *Truth v. Justice: The Morality of Truth*, ed. Robert I. Rotbery and Dennis Thompson (Princeton, NJ: Princeton University Press, 2000). Also see Lucy Allais, "Restorative Justice, Retributive Justice, and the South African Truth and Reconciliation Commission," *Philosophy and Public Affairs* 39, no. 4 (2011); Jonathan Allen, "Between Retribution and Restoration: Justice and the TRC (South Africa's Truth and Reconciliation Commission)," *South African Journal of Philosophy* 20, no. 1 (2001); Charles Villa-Vicencio, "Why Perpetrators Should Not Always Be Prosecuted: Where the International Criminal Court and Truth Commissions Meet," *Emory Law Journal* 49, no. 1 (2000); and Christopher Bennett, "Is Amnesty a Collective Act of Forgiveness?," *Contemporary Political Theory* 2, no. 1 (2003).

26. Thomas Brudholm, *Resentment's Virtue: Jean Améry and the Refusal to Forgive* (Philadelphia: Temple University Press, 2008), 29–30.

27. Truth and Reconciliation Commission, *Report* (1998), vol. 1, chap. 1, para 71.

28. Brudholm, in *Resentment's Virtue*, holds this view, and I agree.

29. Margaret Walker, *Moral Repair: Reconstructing Moral Relations after Wrongdoing* (New York: Cambridge University Press, 2006), 99.

30. Carolyn S. Stauffer, "The Sexual Politics of Gender-Based Violence in South Africa: Linking Public and Private Worlds," *Journal for the Sociological Integration of Religion and Society* 5, no. 1 (2015): 122.

31. Truth and Reconciliation Commission, *Report* (1998), 1:111.

32. Annelies Verdoolaege, "Managing Reconciliation at the Human Rights Violations Hearings of the South African TRC," *Journal of Human Rights* 5, no. 1 (2006): 67.

33. Wilson, *Politics of Truth and Reconciliation*, 120.

34. Brudholm, *Resentment's Virtue*, 30–31.

35. Verdoolaege, *Reconciliation Discourse*, 148.

36. Jeffrey Blustein, *Forgiveness and Remembrance: Remembering Wrongdoing in Personal and Public Life* (New York: Oxford University Press, 2014), 116.

37. Stauffer, "Sexual Politics," 121.

38. Audrey Chapman, "Truth Commissions and Intergroup Forgiveness: The Case of the South African Truth and Reconciliation Commission," *Peace and Conflict: Journal of Peace Psychology* 13, no. 1 (2007).

39. Charles Griswold, *Forgiveness: A Philosophical Exploration* (New York: Cambridge University Press, 2007), 181.

40. This is not to say that all public promotion of forgiveness is necessarily manipulative. However, public promotion of forgiveness risks being manipulative. This is because the state wields more power than the individual.

41. MacLachlan, "The Philosophical Controversy," 45.

42. Maria Mayo, *The Limits of Forgiveness: Case Studies in the Distortion of a Biblical Ideal* (Minneapolis: Fortress Press, 2015), 122.

43. Marilyn McCord Adams, "Forgiveness: A Christian Model," *Faith and Philosophy: Journal of the Society of Christian Philosophers* 8, no. 3 (1991).

44. Thomas Brudholm and Arne Grøn, "Picturing Forgiveness after Atrocity," *Studies in Christian Ethics* 24, no. 2 (2011):159–70.

45. Mayo, *The Limits of Forgiveness*, 132.

46. For more on criticisms of using exemplars to encourage people to forgive, see Myisha Cherry, "Forgiveness, Exemplars, and the Oppressed," in *The Moral Psychology of Forgiveness*, ed. Kathryn J. Norlock (Lanham, MD: Rowman and Littlefield International, 2017).

CHAPTER 5: WHEN RACE MATTERS

1. BBC, "Trayvon Martin's Parents on Path to Forgive George Zimmerman," BBC .com, August 24, 2013, https://www.bbc.com/news/world-us-canada-23822998.

2. CNN Newsroom, "Campus Cop Murder," July 29, 2015, 2:00 p.m., http://www .cnn.com/TRANSCRIPTS/1507/29/cnr.05.html.

3. Forgiveness is thought to be a feminine virtue and is socially expected of women. As a result, women will most likely also be recipients of these requests.

4. The requester might make a quick public request because they see it as preventive—a call to curb violence. The thought is that if the requester quickly makes the request, then racial violence will not quickly ensue. Quick requests for forgiveness could also be tactical—a strategic retreat so the relevant actors can fight another day. Black elites might make the request of other Blacks knowing that if riots occurred, police presence would increase and this would cause economic problems for the community. A sincere forgiveness request could be made as something expressed in public to bring the temperature down and not as a request for them to actually forgive.

5. Judy Eaton, C. Ward Struthers, and Alexander G. Santelli, "The Mediating Role of Perceptual Validation in the Repentance–Forgiveness Process," *Personality and Social Psychology Bulletin* 32, no. 10 (2006): 1398.

6. We might also conclude that forgiveness will have this effect when the request lacks responses like these, although we will need more studies to empirically back up this claim.

7. David Masci, Besheer Mohamed, and Gregory A. Smith, "Black Americans Are More Likely than Overall Public to Be Christian, Protestant," Pew Research Center,

April 23, 2018, https://www.pewresearch.org/fact-tank/2018/04/23/black-americans-are-more-likely-than-overall-public-to-be-christian-protestant/.

8. Robin DiAngelo, *White Fragility: Why It's So Hard for White People to Talk about Racism* (Boston: Beacon Press, 2018).

9. Richard Dyer, *White: Essays on Race and Culture* (New York: Routledge, 1997).

10. OSV Weekly Editorial Board, "'Hate Won't Win': A Message of Love and Forgiveness Stands in Contrast to the Act That Took Nine Lives in Charleston," *OSV Weekly*, June 24, 2015, https://www.osv.com/OSVNewsweekly/Article/TabId/535/ArtMID/13567/ArticleID/17731/Editorial-%E2%80%98Hate-won%E2%80%99t-win%E2%80%99.aspx.

11. Danielle Allen, *Talking to Strangers: Anxieties of Citizenship since Brown v. Board of Education* (Chicago: University of Chicago Press, 2004), 41.

CHAPTER 6: HOME IMPROVEMENT

1. Philosophers disagree as to what exactly grounds these reasons. A view in opposition to Wallace's can be found in Harry G. Frankfurt, *Necessity, Volition, and Love* (Cambridge: Cambridge University Press, 1999), 155–80.

2. R. Jay Wallace, "Duties of Love," *Proceedings of the Aristotelian Society*, suppl. vol. 86, no. 1 (2012): 176.

3. A more detailed argument for the value of anger can be found in Myisha Cherry, *The Case for Rage* (New York: Oxford University Press, 2021).

4. To understand the full argument presented here, see Cherry, *The Case for Rage*.

5. Myisha Cherry, "Love, Anger, and Racial Justice," in *The Routledge Handbook of Love in Philosophy*, ed. Adrianne Martin (New York: Routledge, 2019).

6. For a description of what it means to forgive someone for who they are, see Macalester Bell, "Forgiving Someone for Who They Are (and Not Just What They've Done)," *Philosophy and Phenomenological Research* 77, no. 3 (2008).

7. Paul Coleman, "The Process of Forgiveness in Marriage and Family," in *Exploring Forgiveness*, ed. Robert D. Enright and Joanna North (Madison: University of Wisconsin Press, 1998).

8. Samuel Fleischacker, *Being Me, Being You* (Chicago: University of Chicago Press, 2019), 9.

9. Fleischacker, *Being Me, Being You*, 12.

10. For more on the distinction between prudential considerations and moral considerations, see Samuel Stoljar, "Moral and Prudential Considerations," in *Moral and Legal Reasoning* (London: Palgrave Macmillan, 1980).

11. Joseph Elder, "Expanding Our Options: The Challenge of Forgiveness," in *Exploring Forgiveness*, ed. Robert D. Enright and Joanna North (Madison: University of Wisconsin Press, 1998), 155.

208 NOTES TO CHAPTER 7

12. See Joan Tronto, "Creating Caring Institutions: Politics, Plurality, and Purpose," *Ethics and Social Welfare* 4, no. 2 (2010): 158–71; and Joan C. Tronto and Berenice Fisher, "Toward a Feminist Theory of Caring," in *Circles of Care*, ed. Emily K. Abel and Margaret K. Nelson (Albany: SUNY Press, 1990), 36–54.

CHAPTER 7: THE BUSINESS OF FORGIVENESS

1. James Kerr, "10 Reasons to Forgive a Colleague This Holiday Season," Inc.com (2016), https://www.inc.com/james-kerr/10-reasons-to-forgive-a-colleague-this-holiday-season.html; Jessica Stillman, "When You Should Forgive Your Work Nemesis, according to Science," Inc.com (2016), https://www.inc.com/jessica-stillman/why-you-should-forgive-your-work-nemesis-according-to-science.html.

2. Patrick Proctor, "How to Muster Your Comeback after Letting People Down," Entreprenuer.com, July 6, 2016, https://www.entrepreneur.com/article/271216.

3. Judith Carr-Rodriguez, "Creating Brand Joy, Disrupting with Purpose," Entreprenuer.com, August 19, 2014, https://www.entrepreneur.com/article/236037.

4. Michael Stone, "Forgiveness in the Workplace," *Industrial and Commercial Training* 34, no. 7 (2002): 280.

5. Ryan Fehr and Michelle Gelfand, "The Forgiving Organization: A Multilevel Model of Forgiveness at Work," *Academy of Management Review* 37, no. 4 (2012).

6. Stone, "Forgiveness in the Workplace," 283.

7. Loren Toussaint et al., "Forgiveness Working: Forgiveness, Health, and Productivity in the Workplace," *American Journal of Health Promotion* 32, no. 1 (2016).

8. Toussaint et al., "Forgiveness Working," 8.

9. Loren Toussaint, Frederic Luskin, and Arthur DeLorenzo, "Is Forgiveness One of the Secrets to Success?," *American Journal of Health Promotion* 33, no. 7 (2019).

10. Toussaint et al., "Secrets to Success?"

11. These nine steps are referred to as the "Forgive for Good" method tested by the Stanford Forgiveness Project and explained in Frederic Luskin, *Forgive for Good: A Proven Prescription for Health and Happiness* (New York: HarperOne, 2002).

12. Toussaint et al., "Secrets to Success?," 1092.

13. George H. Litwin and Robert A. Stringer, *Motivation and Organizational Climate* (Cambridge, MA: Harvard University Press, 1968).

14. Toussaint et al., "Forgiveness Working."

15. Plato, *Republic* (Waiheke Island: Floating Press, 2009); L. A. Seneca, *On the Shortness of Life and on the Happy Life* (Manchester, NH: Abbot ePublishing, 2009).

16. Pablo Sanz and Joan Fontrodona, "Moderation as a Moral Competence: Integrating Perspectives for a Better Understanding of Temperance in the Workplace," *Journal of Business Ethics* 155 (2019).

17. Denise Vigani, "Is Patience a Virtue?," *Journal of Value Inquiry* 51, no. 2 (2016).

18. Toussaint et al., "Secrets to Success?"

19. Fehr and Gelfand, "The Forgiving Organization," 665.

20. Christine Porath and Christine Pearson, "The Price of Incivility," *Harvard Business Review* 91, no. 1–2 (2013): 93.

21. Porath and Pearson, "The Price of Incivility," 104.

22. Porath and Pearson, "The Price of Incivility," 100.

23. Porath and Pearson, "The Price of Incivility," 103.

24. Myisha Cherry, "Gendered Failures in Extrinsic Emotional Regulation; Or, Why Telling a Woman to 'Relax' or a Young Boy to 'Stop Crying Like a Girl' Is Not a Good Idea," *Philosophical Topics* 47, no. 2 (2019).

CHAPTER 8: CANCELING VERSUS FORGIVING

1. Jonah Bromwich, "Everyone Is Canceled," *New York Times*, June 28, 2018, https://www.nytimes.com/2018/06/28/style/is-it-canceled.html.

2. Note that when I use the term, I am describing the practice of canceling and not what many refer to as the "mob of cancel culture." I refer to any piling-on acts as one of the vices of canceling.

3. Meredith D. Clark, "Drag Them: A Brief Etymology of So-Called 'Cancel Culture,'" *Communication and the Public* 5, no. 3–4 (2020).

4. Angela Sailor, "Cancel Culture Is against American Value of Forgiveness," *Miami Herald*, July 31, 2020, https://www.miamiherald.com > op-ed > article244633182.

5. Relevant Magazine, "Lizzo's Apology Is a Masterclass in Taking Ownership and Making Things Right," June 14, 2022, https://relevantmagazine.com/culture/music /lizzos-apology-is-a-masterclass-in-taking-ownership-and-making-things-right/.

6. Michelle Peng, "What Workplace Leaders Can Learn from Lizzo's Apology," Time.com, June 24, 2022, https://time.com/charter/6190644/lizzo-apology/.

7. Think of rapper Jay-Z's line from the song "Diamonds from Sierra Leone": "I'm not a businessman, I'm a business man."

8. Clark, "Drag Them," 3.

9. Thomas Hill, "Symbolic Protest and Calculated Silence," *Philosophy and Public Affairs* 9, no. 1 (1979): 99.

10. Joseph Butler, "Sermon VIII. Upon Resentment and Forgiveness of Injuries," http://anglicanhistory.org/butler/rolls/08.html.

11. Charles Griswold, *Forgiveness: A Philosophical Exploration* (New York: Cambridge University Press, 2007), 182.

12. I am persuaded by the philosopher Martha Nussbaum that not all forms of objectification are bad. There can be positive forms. What she has in mind, for

example, are types of objectification that make for a wonderful sexual life for both partners. Here I am instead referring to treating others as objects in objectionable ways. See Nussbaum, "Objectification," *Philosophy and Public Affairs* 24, no. 4 (1995), for more on women and objectification.

CHAPTER 9: FORGIVING YOURSELF

1. Robin Dillon refers to this as forgiving for "wrongdoing, wrong feeling, wishing, wanting, thinking, reacting, and being." See Dillon, "Self-Forgiveness and Self-Respect," *Ethics* 112 (2001): 59.

2. Fyodor Dostoyevsky, *The Brothers Karamazov*, trans. Constance Garnett (New York: Lowell Press, 2021), bk. 7, chap. 4, Gutenberg Archive, https://www.gutenberg.org/files/28054/28054-h/28054-h.htm.

3. Gordon Marino, "The Fantasy of Self-Forgiveness," *Hedgehog Review*, January 4, 2021, https://hedgehogreview.com/web-features/thr/posts/the-fantasy-of-self-forgiveness.

4. See Alice MacLachlan, "Forgiveness and Moral Solidarity," in *Forgiveness: Probing the Boundaries*, ed. Stephen Bloch-Schulman and David Whited (Oxford: Inter-Disciplinary Press, 2009), 3–4.

5. Kathryn Norlock, *Forgiveness from a Feminist Perspective* (Lanham, MD: Lexington Books, 2009), 149.

6. See Susan Brison, *Aftermath: Violence and the Remaking of a Self* (Princeton, NJ: Princeton University Press, 2002), for more on recognizing ourselves as both agents and victims through this process.

7. Sharon Lamb, "Forgiveness Therapy in Gendered Contexts: What Happens to the Truth?," in *Trauma, Truth and Reconciliation*, ed. Nancy Potter (New York: Oxford University Press, 2006), 245.

8. James Baldwin, *The Fire Next Time* (New York: Vintage Books, 1993), 83.

9. Martin Luther King Jr., "A Christmas Sermon on Peace," in *A Testament of Hope*, ed. James Washington (New York: HarperOne, 1986), 254.

10. See MacLachlan, "Forgiveness and Moral Solidarity."

11. In *Forgiveness from a Feminist Perspective*, Norlock refers to this as the "fragmented self."

12. Peter Goldie, *The Mess Inside: Narrative, Emotion, and the Mind* (New York: Oxford University Press, 2012), 106.

13. For a deeper analysis of how third-party forgiveness helps us make sense of self-forgiveness, see Kathryn Norlock, "Why Self-Forgiveness Needs Third-Party Forgiveness," in Bloch-Schulman and Whited, *Forgiveness*.

14. Goldie, *The Mess Inside*, 103.

15. Norlock, *Forgiveness from a Feminist Perspective*, 147.

16. See Alan Gibbard, *Wise Choices, Apt Feelings: A Theory of Normative Judgment* (Cambridge, MA: Harvard University Press, 1990).

17. Will Smith, "It's Been a Minute," YouTube, July 29, 2022, https://www.youtube.com/watch?v=jXrxDKwlA_s.

18. For more on guilt and motivation, see Jesse Prinz and Shaun Nichols, "The Moral Emotions," in *The Moral Psychology Handbook*, ed. John Doris (New York: Oxford University Press, 2012), 132–39.

19. Mary B. Harris, Sheldon M. Benson, and Carroll L. Hall, "The Effects of Confession on Altruism," *Journal of Social Psychology* 96 (1975): 187–92.

20. Norlock, *Forgiveness from a Feminist Perspective*, 147.

21. Norlock, *Forgiveness from a Feminist Perspective*, 150.

22. Dillon, "Self-Forgiveness," 83.

23. Anthony Bash, *Forgiveness and Christian Ethics* (Cambridge: Cambridge University Press, 2007).

24. Espen Gamlund, "Ethical Aspects of Self-Forgiveness," *SATS* 15, no. 2 (2014): 246.

25. Gamlund, "Ethical Aspects," 248–49.

26. Norlock, *Forgiveness from a Feminist Perspective*, 148.

27. Claudia Card, *The Atrocity Paradigm: A Theory of Evil* (New York: Oxford University Press, 2002), 208.

28. Card, *The Atrocity Paradigm*, 169.

29. Card, *The Atrocity Paradigm*, 208.

30. Card, *The Atrocity Paradigm*, 208.

31. Card, *The Atrocity Paradigm*, 208.

32. Norlock, *Forgiveness from a Feminist Perspective*, 153.

33. Card, *The Atrocity Paradigm*, 169.

34. Card, *The Atrocity Paradigm*, 208.

35. Daniel H. Pink, *The Power of Regret* (New York: Riverhead Books, 2022), 129.

36. Norlock, *Forgiveness from a Feminist Perspective*, 153.

37. Omer Mozaffar, "The Caustic Cruelty of Remorse," Roger Ebert.com, May 9, 2012, https://www.rogerebert.com/far-flung-correspondents/the-caustic-cruelty-of-remorse.

CHAPTER 10: RADICAL REPAIR

1. The cars in F1 racing do not have air conditioning because it would be a waste of space and power. The teams choose discomfort in order to increase speed, proving to us that selecting the comfortable option is not always the best choice.

2. Margaret Walker, *Moral Repair: Reconstructing Moral Relations after Wrongdoing* (Cambridge: Cambridge University Press, 2006), 6.

3. Walker, *Moral Repair*, 38.

4. Elizabeth Spelman, *Repair: The Impulse to Restore in a Fragile World* (Boston: Beacon Press, 2002), 72.

5. Corey Irwin, "50 Years Ago: The Pinto Becomes Ford's 'Embarrassment,'" *Ultimate Classic Rock*, September 11, 2020, https://ultimateclassicrock.com/ford -pinto-history/.

6. Al Jazeera, "Lewis Hamilton Overtakes Schumacher with Record 92nd F1 Win," October 25, 2020, https://www.aljazeera.com/news/2020/10/25/hamilton -in-dreamland-after-record-breaking-triumph.

7. Walker, *Moral Repair*, 7.

8. Walker, *Moral Repair*, 19.

9. Walker, *Moral Repair*, 19.

10. Walker, *Moral Repair*, 20.

11. See Kristie Dotson, "Tracking Epistemic Violence, Tracking Practices of Silencing," *Hypatia* 26, no. 2 (2011): 236–57; Cassie Herbert, *Exclusionary Speech and Constructions of Community* (Washington, DC: Georgetown University Press, 2017); Kate Abramson, "Turning Up the Lights on Gaslighting," *Philosophical Perspectives* 28, no. 1 (2014): 1–30.

12. Walker, *Moral Repair*, 20.

13. Walker, *Moral Repair*, 30.

14. Spelman, *Repair*, 5.

15. Michael McCullough, *Beyond Revenge: The Evolution of the Forgiveness Instinct* (San Francisco: Jossey-Bass, 2008), 132.

16. McCullough, *Beyond Revenge*, 126–27.

CONCLUSION

1. Anna Mehler Paperny, "Pope's Apology in Canada Falls Short for Some Indigenous Survivors," Reuters.com, July 27, 2022, https://www.reuters.com/world /americas/popes-apology-canada-falls-short-some-indigenous-survivors-2022-07-27/.

2. Rod Nickel and Phillip Pullella, "Pope Again Asks for Forgiveness as Tour Ends in Canada's North," Reuters.com, July 29, 2022, https://www.reuters.com/world /americas/pope-wraps-up-canadian-apology-tour-with-northern-stop-2022-07-29/.

3. Paperny, "Pope's Apology."

4. Paperny, "Pope's Apology."

5. Paperny, "Pope's Apology."

6. J. McKinley and D. Higgins, "Buffalo Gunman Sentenced to Life in Emotional and Dramatic Hearing," *New York Times*, February 15, 2023, https://www.nytimes .com/2023/02/15/nyregion/buffalo-shooting-gunman-sentencing.html.

REFERENCES

Abramson, Kate. "Turning Up the Lights on Gaslighting." *Philosophical Perspectives* 28, no. 1 (2014).

Adams, Marilyn McCord. "Forgiveness: A Christian Model." *Faith and Philosophy: Journal of the Society of Christian Philosophers* 8, no. 3 (1991).

Al Jazeera. "Lewis Hamilton Overtakes Schumacher with Record 92nd F1 Win." October 25, 2020. https://www.aljazeera.com/news/2020/10/25/hamilton-in -dreamland-after-record-breaking-triumph.

Allais, Lucy. "Restorative Justice, Retributive Justice, and the South African Truth and Reconciliation Commission," *Philosophy and Public Affairs* 39, no. 4 (2011).

Allen, Danielle. *Talking to Strangers: Anxieties of Citizenship since Brown v. Board of Education.* Chicago: University of Chicago Press, 2004.

Allen, Jonathan. "Between Retribution and Restoration: Justice and the TRC (South Africa's Truth and Reconciliation Commission)." *South African Journal of Philosophy* 20, no. 1 (2001).

Baldwin, James. *The Fire Next Time.* New York: Vintage Books, 1993.

Bash, Anthony. *Forgiveness and Christian Ethics.* Cambridge: Cambridge University Press, 2007.

BBC. "Trayvon Martin's Parents on Path to Forgive George Zimmerman." BBC.com . August 24, 2013. https://www.bbc.com/news/world-us-canada-23822998.

Bell, Macalester. "Forgiving Someone for Who They Are (and Not Just What They've Done)." *Philosophy and Phenomenological Research* 77, no. 3 (2008).

———. *Hard Feelings: The Moral Psychology of Contempt.* New York: Oxford University Press, 2013.

Bennett, Christopher. "Is Amnesty a Collective Act of Forgiveness?" *Contemporary Political Theory* 2, no. 1 (2003).

Blustein, Jeffrey. *Forgiveness and Remembrance: Remembering Wrongdoing in Personal and Public Life.* New York: Oxford University Press, 2014.

Brison, Susan. *Aftermath: Violence and the Remaking of a Self.* Princeton, NJ: Princeton University Press, 2002.

Bromwich, Jonah. "Everyone Is Canceled." *New York Times*, June 28, 2018. https://www.nytimes.com/2018/06/28/style/is-it-canceled.html.

Brudholm, Thomas. *Resentment's Virtue: Jean Améry and the Refusal to Forgive*. Philadelphia: Temple University Press, 2008.

Brudholm, Thomas, and Arne Grøn. "Picturing Forgiveness after Atrocity." *Studies in Christian Ethics* 24, no. 2 (2011).

Butler, Joseph. "Sermon VIII. Upon Resentment and Forgiveness of Injuries." http://anglicanhistory.org/butler/rolls/08.html.

Card, Claudia. *The Atrocity Paradigm: A Theory of Evil*. New York: Oxford University Press, 2002.

Carr-Rodriguez, Judith. "Creating Brand Joy: Disrupting with Purpose." Entreprenuer.com, August 19, 2014. https://www.entrepreneur.com/article/236037.

Carse, Alisa L., and Lynne Tirrell. "Forgiving Grave Wrongs." In *Forgiveness in Perspective*, edited by Christopher Allers and Marieke Smit. Amsterdam: Rodopi Press, 2010.

Chapman, Audrey. "Truth Commissions and Intergroup Forgiveness: The Case of the South African Truth and Reconciliation Commission." *Peace and Conflict: Journal of Peace Psychology* 13, no. 1 (2007).

Chapman, Gary, and Jennifer Thomas. *The Five Languages of Apology*. Chicago: Northfield, 2006.

Chappell, Bill, and Richard Gonzales. "Brandt Jean's Act of Grace toward His Brother's Killer Sparks a Debate over Forgiving." NPR, October 3, 2019. https://www.npr.org/2019/10/03/766866875/brandt-jeans-act-of-grace-toward-his-brother-s-killer-sparks-a-debate-over-forgi.

Cherry, Myisha. *The Case for Rage*. New York: Oxford University Press, 2021.

———. "Forgiveness, Exemplars, and the Oppressed." In *The Moral Psychology of Forgiveness*, edited by Kathryn J. Norlock. Lanham, MD: Rowman and Littlefield International, 2017.

———. "Gendered Failures in Extrinsic Emotional Regulation: Or, Why Telling a Woman to 'Relax' or a Young Boy to 'Stop Crying Like a Girl' Is Not a Good Idea." *Philosophical Topics* 47, no. 2 (2019).

———. "Love, Anger, and Racial Justice." In *The Routledge Handbook of Love in Philosophy*, edited by Adrianne Martin. New York: Routledge, 2019.

———. "Racialized Forgiveness." *Hypatia: A Journal of Feminist Philosophy* 36, no. 4 (2021).

Clark, Meredith D. "Drag Them: A Brief Etymology of So-Called 'Cancel Culture.'" *Communication and the Public* 5, no. 3–4 (2020).

CNN Newsroom. "Campus Cop Murder." July 29, 2015. http://www.cnn.com/TRANSCRIPTS/1507/29/cnr.05.html.

Coleman, Paul. "The Process of Forgiveness in Marriage and Family." In *Exploring Forgiveness*, edited by Robert D. Enright and Joanna North. Madison: University of Wisconsin Press, 1998.

Da Silva, Chantal. "'Forgiveness' Is Trending after Moment Botham Jean's Brother Hugged Police Officer Who Killed Him and Told Her: 'I Don't Even Want You to Go to Jail.'" Newsweek.com, October 3, 2019. https://www.newsweek.com /botham-jean-brother-bryant-offers-forgiveness-hug-amber-guyger-dallas -1462868.

DiAngelo, Robin. *White Fragility: Why It's So Hard for White People to Talk about Racism*. Boston: Beacon Press, 2018.

Dillon, Robin. "Self-Forgiveness and Self-Respect." *Ethics* 112 (2001).

Dostoyevsky, Fyodor. *The Brothers Karamazov*. Translated by Constance Garnett. New York: Lowell Press, 2021. Gutenberg Archive. https://www.gutenberg.org /files/28054/28054-h/28054-h.htm.

Dotson, Kristie. "Tracking Epistemic Violence, Tracking Practices of Silencing." *Hypatia: A Journal of Feminist Philosophy* 26, no. 2 (2011).

Dyer, Richard. *White: Essays on Race and Culture*. New York: Routledge, 1997.

Eaton, Judy, C. Ward Struthers, and Alexander G. Santelli. "The Mediating Role of Perceptual Validation in the Repentance–Forgiveness Process." *Personality and Social Psychology Bulletin* 32, no. 10 (2006).

Elder, Joseph. "Expanding Our Options: The Challenge of Forgiveness." In *Exploring Forgiveness*, edited by Robert D. Enright and Joanna North. Madison: University of Wisconsin Press, 1998.

Fehr, Ryan, and Michelle Gelfand. "The Forgiving Organization: A Multilevel Model of Forgiveness at Work." *Academy of Management Review* 37, no. 4 (2012).

Fleischacker, Samuel. *Being Me, Being You*. Chicago: University of Chicago Press, 2019.

Francis, Enjoli, and Bill Hutchinson. "'I Don't Forgive This Woman, and She Needs Help': Black Child Wrongly Accused of Grabbing 'Cornerstore Caroline.'" ABC News, October 16, 2018. https://abcnews.go.com/US/white-woman-apologizes -alleging-black-child-assaulted-york/story?id=58505763.

Frankfurt, Harry G. *Necessity, Volition, and Love*. Cambridge: Cambridge University Press, 1999.

Friedman, Roger. "Widows to Testify at Hearings." Cape Times Independent Online, April 15, 1996. https://www.iol.co.za/.

Gamlund, Espen. "Ethical Aspects of Self-Forgiveness." *SATS* 15, no. 2 (2014): 237–56.

Gibbard, Alan. *Wise Choices, Apt Feelings: A Theory of Normative Judgment*. Cambridge, MA: Harvard University Press, 1990.

Goldie, Peter. *The Mess Inside: Narrative, Emotion, and the Mind.* New York: Oxford University Press, 2012.

Griswold, Charles. *Forgiveness: A Philosophical Exploration.* New York: Cambridge University Press, 2007.

Hampton, Jean. "Forgiveness, Resentment, and Hatred." In *Forgiveness and Mercy,* edited by Jeffrie G. Murphy and Jean Hampton. Cambridge: Cambridge University Press, 1988.

Harris, Mary B., Sheldon M. Benson, and Carroll L. Hall. "The Effects of Confession on Altruism." *Journal of Social Psychology* 96 (1975).

Herbert, Cassie. *Exclusionary Speech and Constructions of Community.* Washington, DC: Georgetown University Press, 2017.

Hill, Thomas. "Symbolic Protest and Calculated Silence." *Philosophy and Public Affairs* 9, no. 1 (1979).

Hunter, Al. "Dr. Martin Luther King, Jr. in Indianapolis, Part 2." *Weekly View,* June 9, 2014. http://weeklyview.net/2014/01/09/dr-martin-luther-king-jr-in-indiana polis-part-2/.

Irwin, Corey. "50 Years Ago: The Pinto Becomes Ford's 'Embarrassment.'" *Ultimate Classic Rock.* September 11, 2020. https://ultimateclassicrock.com/ford-pinto -history/.

Kerr, James. "10 Reasons to Forgive a Colleague This Holiday Season." Inc.com. 2016. https://www.inc.com/james-kerr/10-reasons-to-forgive-a-colleague-this -holiday-season.html.

Khulumani Support Group South Africa. "How the TRC Failed Women in South Africa: A Failure That Has Proved Fertile Ground for the Gender Violence Women in South Africa Face Today." October 3, 2011. http://www.khulumani.netitem/527 -how-the-trc-failed-women-in-south-africa-a-failure-that-has-proved-fertile -ground-for-the-gender-violence-women-in-south-africa-face-today.htm.

King, Martin Luther. "A Christmas Sermon on Peace." In *A Testament of Hope,* edited by James Washington. New York: HarperOne, 1986.

Kiss, Elizabeth. "Moral Ambition within and beyond Political Constraints." In *Truth v. Justice: The Morality of Truth,* edited by Robert I. Rotbery and Dennis Thompson. Princeton, NJ: Princeton University Press, 2000.

Kohen, Ari. "The Person and the Political: Forgiveness and Reconciliation in Restorative Justice." *Critical Review of International Social and Political Philosophy* 12, no. 3 (2009).

Lamb, Sharon. "Forgiveness Therapy in Gendered Contexts: What Happens to the Truth?" In *Trauma, Truth and Reconciliation,* edited by Nancy Potter. New York: Oxford University Press, 2006.

Leman-Langlois, Stéphane, and Clifford D. Shearing. "Repairing the Future: The South African Truth and Reconciliation Commission at Work." In *Crime, Truth and Justice: Official Inquiry, Discourse, Knowledge,* edited by George Gilligan and John Pratt. Cullompton, UK: Willan, 2004.

Litwin, George H., and Robert A. Stringer. *Motivation and Organizational Climate.* Cambridge, MA: Harvard University Press, 1968.

Luskin, Frederic. *Forgive for Good: A Proven Prescription for Health and Happiness.* New York: HarperOne, 2002.

MacLachlan, Alice. "Authoritative Norms and Internal Goods: The Normativity of Moral Practices." Manuscript. 2015.

―――. "Forgiveness and Moral Solidarity." In *Forgiveness: Probing the Boundaries,* edited by Stephen Bloch-Schulman and David Whited. Oxford: Inter-Disciplinary Press, 2009.

―――. "Gender and Public Apology." *Transitional Justice Review* 1, no. 2 (2013).

―――. "The Philosophical Controversy over Political Forgiveness." In *Public Forgiveness in Post-Conflict Contexts,* edited by Paul van Tongeren, Neelke Doorn, and Bas van Stokkom. Cambridge: Intersentia, 2012.

―――. "Practicing Imperfect Forgiveness." In *Feminist Ethics and Social and Political Philosophy: Theorizing the Non-Ideal,* edited by Lisa Tessman. Dordrecht: Springer, 2009.

Marino, Gordon. "The Fantasy of Self-Forgiveness." *Hedgehog Review,* January 4, 2021. https://hedgehogreview.com/web-features/thr/posts/the-fantasy-of-self-forgiveness.

Masci, David, Besheer Mohamed, and Gregory A. Smith. "Black Americans Are More Likely than Overall Public to Be Christian, Protestant." Pew Research Center, April 23, 2018. https://www.pewresearch.org/fact-tank/2018/04/23/black-americans-are-more-likely-than-overall-public-to-be-christian-protestant/.

Mayo, Maria. *The Limits of Forgiveness: Case Studies in the Distortion of a Biblical Ideal.* Minneapolis: Fortress Press, 2015.

McCullough, Michael. *Beyond Revenge: The Evolution of the Forgiveness Instinct.* San Francisco: Jossey-Bass, 2008.

McKinley, J., and D. Higgins. "Buffalo Gunman Sentenced to Life in Emotional and Dramatic Hearing." *New York Times,* February 15, 2023. https://www.nytimes.com/2023/02/15/nyregion/buffalo-shooting-gunman-sentencing.html.

Minow, Martha. *Between Vengeance and Forgiveness: Facing History after Genocide and Mass Violence.* Boston: Beacon Press, 1998.

―――. "Forgiveness, Law, and Justice." *California Law Review* 103, no. 6 (2015).

Mozaffar, Omer. "The Caustic Cruelty of Remorse." Roger Ebert.com, May 9, 2012. https://www.rogerebert.com/far-flung-correspondents/the-caustic-cruelty-of-remorse.

Murphy, Jeffrie G. *Getting Even: Forgiveness and Its Limits.* New York: Oxford University Press, 2003.

Nagel, Thomas. "Concealment and Exposure." *Philosophy and Public Affairs* 27, no. 1 (1998).

National Unity and Reconciliation Act, Section (3) (1). *Government Gazette* 361, no. 16579 (July 26, 1995).

Nickel, Rod, and Phillip Pullella. "Pope Again Asks for Forgiveness as Tour Ends in Canada's North." Reuters.com, July 29, 2022. https://www.reuters.com/world /americas/pope-wraps-up-canadian-apology-tour-with-northern-stop-2022-07 -29/.

Norlock, Kathryn. *Forgiveness from a Feminist Perspective.* Lanham, MD: Lexington Books, 2009.

———. "Why Self-Forgiveness Needs Third-Party Forgiveness." In *Forgiveness: Probing the Boundaries,* edited by Stephen Bloch-Schulman and David Whited. Oxford: Inter-Disciplinary Press, 2009.

Nussbaum, Martha. *Anger and Forgiveness.* New York: Oxford University Press, 2016.

———. "Objectification." *Philosophy and Public Affairs* 24, no. 4 (1995).

OSV Weekly Editorial Board. "'Hate Won't Win': A Message of Love and Forgiveness Stands in Contrast to the Act That Took Nine Lives in Charleston." *OSV Weekly,* June 24, 2015. https://www.osv.com/OSVNewsweekly/Article/TabId/535/Art MID/13567/ArticleID/17731/Editorial-%E2%80%98Hate-won%E2%80%99t -win%E2%80%99.aspx.

Paperny, Anna Mehler. "Pope's Apology in Canada Falls Short for Some Indigenous Survivors." Reuters.com. July 27, 2022. https://www.reuters.com/world/americas /popes-apology-canada-falls-short-some-indigenous-survivors-2022-07-27/.

Peng, Michelle. "What Workplace Leaders Can Learn from Lizzo's Apology." Time .com, June 24, 2022. https://time.com/charter/6190644/lizzo-apology/.

Pink, Daniel H. *The Power of Regret.* New York: Riverhead Books, 2022.

Plato. *Republic.* Waiheke Island: Floating Press, 2009.

Porath, Christine, and Christine Pearson. "The Price of Incivility." *Harvard Business Review* 91, no. 1–2 (2013).

Prinz, Jesse, and Shaun Nichols. "The Moral Emotions." In *The Moral Psychology Handbook,* edited by John Doris. New York: Oxford University Press, 2012.

Proctor, Patrick. "How to Muster Your Comeback after Letting People Down." En- treprenuer.com, July 6, 2016. https://www.entrepreneur.com/article/271216.

Radzik, Linda, and Colleen Murphy. "Reconciliation." In *Stanford Encyclopedia of Philosophy.* 2015. https://plato.stanford.edu/.

Relevant Magazine. "Lizzo's Apology Is a Masterclass in Taking Ownership and Making Things Right." June 14, 2022. https://relevantmagazine.com/culture /music/lizzos-apology-is-a-masterclass-in-taking-ownership-and-making-things -right/.

Sailor, Angela. "Cancel Culture Is against American Value of Forgiveness." *Miami Herald*, July 31, 2020. https://www.miamiherald.com > op-ed > article244633182.

Sanz, Pablo, and Joan Fontrodona. "Moderation as a Moral Competence: Integrating Perspectives for a Better Understanding of Temperance in the Workplace." *Journal of Business Ethics*155 (2019): 981–94.

Schwarzenegger Pratt, Katherine. *The Gift of Forgiveness: Inspiring Stories from Those Who Have Overcome the Unforgivable.* New York: Penguin Books, 2021.

Seneca, Lucius Annaeus. *On the Shortness of Life and on the Happy Life.* Manchester, NH: Abbot ePublishing, 2009.

Simon, Darran, Ed Lavandera, and Ashley Killough. "His Hug of Forgiveness Shocked the Country. Yet He Still Won't Watch the Video from That Moment." CNN.com. December 8, 2019. https://www.cnn.com/2019/12/06/us/brandt-jean-botham-jean-forgiveness/index.html.

Smith, Will. "It's Been a Minute." YouTube, July 29, 2022. https://www.youtube.com/watch?v=jXrxDKwlA_s.

Spelman, Elizabeth. *Repair: The Impulse to Restore in a Fragile World.* Boston: Beacon Press, 2002.

Stauffer, Carolyn S. "The Sexual Politics of Gender-Based Violence in South Africa: Linking Public and Private Worlds." *Journal for the Sociological Integration of Religion and Society* 5, no. 1 (2015).

Stillman, Jessica. "When You Should Forgive Your Work Nemesis, according to Science." Inc.com. 2016. https://www.inc.com/jessica-stillman/why-you-should-forgive-your-work-nemesis-according-to-science.html.

Stoljar, Samuel. "Moral and Prudential Considerations." In *Moral and Legal Reasoning.* London: Palgrave Macmillan, 1980.

Stone, Michael. "Forgiveness in the Workplace." *Industrial and Commercial Training* 34, no. 7 (2002).

Szablowinski, Zenon. "Apology with and without a Request for Forgiveness." *Heythrop Journal* 53, no. 5 (2012).

Tornielli, Andrea. "Gun Shots, Fear, Prayer and Forgiveness." *Vatican News*, May 14, 2021. https://www.vaticannews.va/en/pope/news/2021-05/gun-shots-fear-prayer-and-forgiveness.html.

Toussaint, Loren, et al. "Forgiveness Working: Forgiveness, Health, and Productivity in the Workplace." *American Journal of Health Promotion* 32, no. 1 (2016).

Toussaint, Loren, Frederic Luskin, and Arthur DeLorenzo. "Is Forgiveness One of the Secrets to Success?" *American Journal of Health Promotion* 33, no. 7 (2019).

Tronto, Joan. "Creating Caring Institutions: Politics, Plurality, and Purpose." *Ethics and Social Welfare* 4, no. 2 (2010).

Tronto, Joan C., and Berenice Fisher. "Toward a Feminist Theory of Caring." In *Circles of Care*, edited by Emily K. Abel and Margaret K. Nelson. Albany: SUNY Press, 1990.

Truth and Reconciliation Commission. "Amnesty Hearings, Date: July 8, 1997, Name: Mongesi Christopher Manquina." 1997. http://www.justice.gov.za/trc/amntrans%5Ccapetown/capetown_biehl01.htm.

———. "Day 3—24 April 1996, Case No: CT/00205, Victim: Nomatise Evelyn Tsobileyo, Violation: Serious Injuries, Testimony from: Nomatise Evelyn Tsobileyo." 1996. http://www.justice.gov.za/trc/hrvtrans%5Cheide/ct00205.htm.

———. "Human Rights Violations, Submissions—Questions and Answers, Date: 12 May 1997, Name: Nomakhosazana Gladys Papu." 1997. http://www.justice.gov.za/trc/hrvtrans%5Ckwtown/papu.htm.

———. "Human Rights Violations, Submissions—Questions and Answers, Date: 10th June 1997, Name: Mrs Bernice Elizabeth Whitefield." 1997. http://www.justice.gov.za/trc/hrvtrans%5Chrvel2/elnwhi.htm.

———. *Truth and Reconciliation Commission of South Africa Report.* 1998. http://www.justice.gov.za/trc/report/finalreport/Volume%201.pdf.

Tutu, Desmond. *No Future without Forgiveness.* London: Random House, 1999.

van Tongeren, Paul, Neelke Doorn, and Bas van Stokkom, eds. *Public Forgiveness in Post-Conflict Contexts.* Cambridge: Intersentia, 2012.

Verdoolaege, Annelies. "Managing Reconciliation at the Human Rights Violations Hearings of the South African TRC." *Journal of Human Rights* 5, no. 1 (2006).

———. *Reconciliation Discourse: The Case of the Truth and Reconciliation Commission.* Volume 27 of *Discourse Approaches to Politics, Society, and Culture.* Philadelphia: John Benjamins, 2008.

Vigani, Denise. "Is Patience a Virtue?" *Journal of Value Inquiry* 51, no. 2 (2016).

Villa-Vicencio, Charles. "Why Perpetrators Should Not Always Be Prosecuted: Where the International Criminal Court and Truth Commissions Meet." *Emory Law Journal* 49, no. 1 (2000).

Walker, Margaret. *Moral Repair: Reconstructing Moral Relations after Wrongdoing.* New York: Cambridge University Press, 2006.

Wallace, R. Jay. "Duties of Love." *Proceedings of the Aristotelian Society*, suppl. vol. 86, no. 1 (2012).

Williamson, Ian, Marti Hope Gonzales, Sierra Fernandez, and Allison Williams. "Forgiveness Aversion: Developing a Motivational State Measure of Perceived Forgiveness Risks." *Motivation and Emotion* 38, no. 3 (2013).

Wilson, Richard A. *The Politics of Truth and Reconciliation in South Africa: Legitimizing the Post-Apartheid State.* Cambridge: Cambridge University Press, 2001.

INDEX

Abramson, Kate, 183
accountability, 141–43, 145, 149, 151,
    183
Ali, Muhammad, 141
Allen, Danielle, 94
Anawak, Jack, 192
anger, 2, 4; anger eradicators, 12, 13, 19;
    anger moderators, 13; defense of, 5;
    letting go of, 9–10, 11, 73, 74, 103;
    process problem and, 101, 102–3;
    projected onto others, 10; as protest,
    31; revenge and, 74
apologies, 17, 28, 202n8; added to
    requests for forgiveness, 59–62; by
    celebrities, 143; lack of, 40; of Pope
    Francis to Indigenous Canadians,
    191–94; as "vice nested in virtue,"
    59–60; by Zimmerman, 85

Baldwin, James, 46, 47, 160
Bash, Anthony, 166
Blacks: agency of Black victims, 89, 93;
    Black men stereotypically perceived
    as threatening, 58–59; Black women,
    93, 141; boycotts of civil rights move-
    ment, 144, 145; as perpetrators, 88–89,
    90; as victims of hate crimes, 85
Brooks, Cornell, 36
Brothers Karamazov, The (Dostoyevsky),
    157–58

bullying, in workplace, 122,
    123–24
Butler, Joseph, 5, 15, 18, 149–50

Calata, Nomonde, 71
"cancel culture," 139, 147–50, 209n2
canceling, 138–39; accountability and,
    141; of celebrities, 141–43; meeting
    point of transactions and morality,
    140–46; mercy/forgiveness culture
    versus cancel culture, 146–51; in
    private, 151–55
Card, Claudia, 169–72
Castile, Philando, 86
celebrities, canceling of, 140–43, 148,
    149, 155, 194
Chapman, Gary, 49
Chappelle, Dave, 139
Charleston massacre (2015), 1–4, 31,
    43–44, 81; families' forgiveness of
    Roof, 113; media coverage of,
    93–94
Christianity, 4, 66–67, 70; of Black
    victims, 89–90; Catholic Church
    abuse of Indigenous Canadians,
    191–94; Christian exclusivity in
    TRC, 78–81; Jesus as exemplar of
    forgiveness, 80
civility, in workplace, 132–33
civil rights movement, 144, 145

221

withholders, 40–45; mercy and, 147; pressure/coercion to forgive and, 39–40; repair and, 195–96; unreadiness to forgive and, 38–39
Forgiveness and Mercy (Hampton), 14
forgivers, 2, 5, 12, 21, 26; conditions of forgiveness and, 29; defended against critics, 31–37; as "moral superheroes," 43; responsibility of communication and, 35; self-focused and other-focused, 30
Formula One Racing, radical repair and, 173–74, 180, 181–82, 187, 211n1
Francis, Pope, 191–94
Franklin, DeVon, 10, 12, 23

Gamlund, Espen, 166–67
Gandhi, Mohandas K., 80
Garner, Eric, 83–84
Garner, Esaw, 83–84
gaslighting, 40, 184
Gelfand, Michele, 129
gender, 58, 95, 183–84; apologies and gendered expectations, 61; hierarchy of, 93; social power and, 127; stereotypes, 33, 135; "testimonial injustice" and, 183
Giovanni's Room (Baldwin), 46–47
Goldie, Peter, 162–63
goodwill extenders, 15
gossip, 17, 24, 38
grief, 7–8, 156
Griswold, Charles, 5, 150
Grit (Duckworth), 135
guilt, 163–64
Guyger, Amber, 35

Hamilton, Sir Lewis, 181–82
Hampton, Jean, 14
Harris, Mary B., 164
Harry, Prince, 98–99

Hart, Kevin, 139
Harvey, Jeremiah, 27–28, 37, 40, 44, 45
hatred, 1–2, 3, 12; hate crimes, 85; letting go of, 11, 14; thwarted by forgiveness, 30–31
healing process, 30, 57, 83, 85, 97, 193, 204n21; empowerment of victims and, 70; family conflicts and, 100; lopsided forgiveness requests and, 94; moral practice of forgiveness and, 37; psychological markers and, 85; TRC (Truth and Reconciliation Commission) and, 76
Herbert, Cassie, 183
Hill, Thomas, 145–46
Hollywood films, 3, 60, 105
Human Rights Violations committee (HRV), 64–65
hurry-and-bury ritual, 84–88, 89, 91–92, 93, 95, 97; climate of respectful cooperation and, 135; dark side of forgiveness and, 125–26; impatience for forgiveness and, 108

Indigenous people, of Canada, 191–93
inquiries, for forgiveness, 48; check-ins, 50, 53–55; introspective, 50, 52–53, 63; predictive, 50–52, 62, 63

Jean, Botham, 35
Jean, Brandt, 35–36, 44
Joanne the Scammer (fictional character), 138, 151
John Paul II, Pope, 10–11, 13
Johnson, Michal, 88–89
Joseph, Frederick, 35
journalists, 4, 6, 64, 139, 143

King, Martin Luther, Jr., 11, 13, 15, 24, 80, 146; on the network of mutuality, 160; as a radical, 176

shame, 112, 191; guilt compared with, 163, 164; protection problem and, 115; self-forgiveness and, 157, 163; sexuality and, 47, 142; withholding of forgiveness and, 45
Smith, Will, 163
social media, 3, 17, 47, 145, 159, 174
Spacey, Kevin, 60–61
Spelman, Elizabeth, 181, 186, 188
Stone, Michael, 119
Szablowinski, Zenon, 61

Talking to Strangers (Allen), 94
temperance, as cultural value, 122, 124–25, 132, 134
therapy, 125, 150, 194
Thomas, Jennifer, 49
Thompson, Anthony, 1, 3
Thompson, Myra, 1
Tokyo Story (film, dir. Ozu, 1953), 113–14
Too Soon Norm, 86, 87, 97
Toussaint, Loren, 129
trauma, 38, 112, 192
TRC (Truth and Reconciliation Commission), South African, 64–65, 81–82, 96, 139; Christian exclusivity and, 78–81; critics of, 72–75, 204n25; forced forgiveness and, 75–78; history of, 65–69; "non-ideal testifiers," 76–77; value of forgiveness and, 69–72; women as testifiers, 67–69, 203n13
trust, rebuilding of, 22, 108
Tutu, Archbishop Desmond, 66, 69, 71, 74, 77, 80

vengeance. See revenge/vengeance
Verdoolaege, Annelies, 76, 204n25
victims: acknowledgment of, 72, 88, 184; agency of, 45, 49, 50, 55, 75, 95;

autonomy of, 69, 70; commands to forgive and, 49–50; disrespect toward, 7; empowerment of, 70; false choice presented to by TRC, 72–75; healing for, 57; letting go of hatred by, 14–15; pleas for forgiveness and, 55; power taken from by wrongdoers, 51; privacy of, 55; repentance of wrongdoers and, 167; requests for forgiveness and, 47–48; victim–perpetrator relationship, 22, 32; of violent crime, 11
violence, 3, 72, 94, 143, 159; genocidal, 80; hate-based, 179; racial, 84, 86, 87, 206n4; state, 81. See also police brutality

wait-and-relate principle, 108–11
Walker, Margaret, 74, 180–81, 182–83
Wallace, R. Jay, 99
Weinstein, Harvey, 142
West, Kanye, 139, 142
"What if" game, 164–65
Williamson, Ian, 38, 39
Wilson, Richard A., 76, 204n25
Winfrey, Oprah, 98, 116
women: anger and, 133; Black women, 93, 141; canceling of, 151–52; forgiveness expected of, 61, 84, 206n3; gender stereotypes and, 33; protection problem and, 112; suffragists as radicals, 176; as TRC testifiers, 67–69, 203n13. See also misogyny
workplace, forgiveness in, 136–37, 196; climate of respectful cooperation and, 131–36, 137; conflicts satirized in The Office, 117–18; cultural values and, 121–25; "culture of forgiveness," 118; dark side of, 125–27; forgiveness as secret to success, 118–21;